UNIVERSITY FOR
A GOOD WOMAN

Kaelie Giffel

UNIVERSITY FOR
A GOOD WOMAN

Reflections on Gender, Class, and Labor in American Higher Education

The Gender Studies Collection

Collection Editors

Jan Etienne & Reham El Morally

LPp

First published in 2024 by Lived Places Publishing

The author and editors have made every effort to ensure the accuracy of information contained in this publication, but assume no responsibility for any errors, inaccuracies, inconsistencies, and omissions. Likewise, every effort has been made to contact copyright holders. If any copyright material has been reproduced unwittingly and without permission the Publisher will gladly receive information enabling them to rectify any error or omission in subsequent editions.

British Library Cataloguing in Publication Data
A CIP record for this book is available from the British Library

ISBN: 9781916704978 (pbk)
ISBN: 9781916704992 (ePDF)
ISBN: 9781916704985 (ePUB)

The right of Kaelie Giffel to be identified as the Author of this work has been asserted by them in accordance with the Copyright, Design and Patents Act 1988.

Cover design by Fiachra McCarthy
Book design by Rachel Trolove of Twin Trail Design
Typeset by Newgen Publishing UK

Lived Places Publishing
Long Island
New York 11789

www.livedplacespublishing.com

Abstract

Drawing from her own experiences in American universities, author Kaelie Giffel explores the university's role in producing inequality. Exploring the intersections of gender, labor, and class, *University for a Good Woman: Reflections on Gender, Class, and Labor in American Higher Education* follows Kaelie through experiences of harassment, overwork, struggles against voicelessness, union organizing, and navigating silent, classed expectations about professionalism and research. Kaelie argues that feminists can and should engage in remaking the university, analyzing places for intervention and transformation.

Providing an important critique of the university and its "post-feminist" narrative, this book is ideal reading for students of feminism, gender studies, critical university studies, education studies, and sociology, as well as graduate mentors, university administrators, and DEIB offices.

Key words

Education; United States; lived experience; misogyny; patriarchy; inequality; harassment; overwork; voicelessness; union organizing

Acknowledgments

There are so many people to thank for supporting me through writing this book, at all stages. Thank you to Lived Places Publishing, especially Jan Etienne, Reham El Morally, and David Parker. This book wouldn't exist without their kindness and patience as I wrote this, my first book. My mentors, Stephanie Clare and Juliet Shields, made this book possible. Gratitude to Renee Lynch for our weekly accountability meetings and gently crushing our goals. So much appreciation Kathleen Reeves for all our conversations about feminism and the thinking life. Thank you to Reuven Pinnata for so many conversations about this book, graduate school, and what it means to be a thinker. Many thanks to Caitlin Postal for our collaborations, leading me to more critical thinking about the university.

My UAW 4121 siblings, Sam Sumpter and Paige Sechrest, taught me all I know about union organizing, power, and the university. My friends, students, and co-workers at the North Carolina State Women's Center who made my final years in the university feel worthwhile: Fiona Prestemon, Lily Smith, Makenzie Rink, Ruby Hernandez, Antoinette Norton, and Carly Woolard. And to my longest friend from university, Leslie Pearson, you've been with me every step of my intellectual journey.

My parents, Deanna and Nicholas Giffel, valued education for me and my siblings and always encouraged me to do what felt right, even if it looked strange to others. My sisters, Kaira Giffel, Kynlee

Giffel, and Kegyn Jordan, remind me how fun life is when I feel too consumed by work. I also want to thank my mother-in-law, Robin Stephens, for her enthusiasm at every stage of my writing, and for always asking me how the writing is going. My grandparents, Terry and Robert Giffel and Barbara and Craig Williams, who always gave me a place to stay while traveling and cheered me on along my educational journey.

My two dogs also supported me through the emotionally difficult process of graduate school and the writing of this book. Many thanks to Remy, who died as I wrote this manuscript, and Sylvia, who still cuddles and snores. They made sure I didn't forget to go outside and reminded me that working all the time is not a natural phenomenon.

Finally, endless thanks and love to my partner, Zachary Cook, who has supported me since I decided to go to graduate school and has held me to my writing dreams for over a decade. Sometimes I take for granted when you say, "You can do it!" But I know not everyone has that kind of love, belief and encouragement. I could not have done this without you.

Contents

Learning objectives

1. Demonstrate the different dynamics of gender, labor, and class within the university, including how they overlap, diverge, and interact.

2. Analyze the different positions of power within a university and identify how these positions rely on inequality.

3. Understand dominant narratives about education and how they erase the reality of social inequality.

4. Identify places within a university that could be changed by individuals or through collective action.

5. Encourage better culture in universities by raising awareness about individual participation in harmful behaviors such as misogyny, racism, and classism.

6. Challenge hierarchy alongside others by sharing experiences and identifying weaknesses in the power structure.

Preface

"Well," my committee member said, "graduate school is supposed to be hard."

Pause. What to say?

"Not this hard," I said.

I think about this conversation a lot. I think about the failure of my interlocutor. I couldn't explain why I had a terrible time in graduate school. I wrote a dissertation that railed against its injustices. Unfortunately, the dissertation was a convoluted project. After I finished it, I still had difficulty explaining my experience. My dissertation was an initial attempt to formulate, in the words of other writers, what was wrong. This book attempts to explain that experience in my own voice.

University for a Good Woman: Reflections on Gender, Class, and Labor in American Higher Education is about my experience of higher education. I hope this book is helpful to anyone in the university. Whether you are suffering similar problems or supporting those who are, I hope you find some solace here. I thought of students, faculty, and staff who may have had similar experiences. I detail harassment, misogyny, overwork, and the struggle for a voice. I write about the ways the university failed me. I write about the things I loved about my education, too.

I didn't write this book just to share my experience. I also wrote this book to share strategies for changing the university. I wanted to show the changes we could make for the better. I wanted to show change over long and short timescales. I also wanted to tell my union organizing story. You don't have to have a union to make change, however. Most movements for change start simply: by talking with people you know. Find out if your classmates noticed the terrible aspects of a particular class. Ask coworkers how their managers are treating them. Then decide, together, what you can do about it.

The university is not organized for the benefit of most people. However, we can change things. It just won't be quick. Or pretty. Struggles over how to define a university involve other forces. Take the current attack on DEI and identity-based departments. State legislatures have attacked teaching and talking about identity or oppression. Why? It does not benefit the ruling class to have politically conscious workers. By controlling knowledge production, they can depoliticize us. They can also pit us against one another. Oppression is not having access to the knowledge you need when you need it.

It's important to understand that universities are not just made of classrooms. Universities are a site of power within the market. They produce skilled workers in a variety of ways. They also employ them. They collaborate with the military. Universities are involved in governments in the US and abroad. They fund innovative thinking in disciplines, albeit unevenly. They police their students and suppress their speech. Keeping these things in mind expands what we mean when we say "university." It also provides different avenues for critique.

I use power analysis throughout the book. Power analysis is a way of thinking I learned in union organizing. It begins with individual testimony. Then it considers the structural factors of a problem. Turning toward solutions, it identifies what we need to challenge. Making change is difficult, however. Sometimes knowing who or what to challenge does not mean we know how. It doesn't mean we'll be successful if we try. Universities, like all power structures, do not change willingly. Universities should be accountable to the students and workers that make it possible. Instead, they seem to care more about their respective boards of governors and wealthy alumni. It is wrong that a small group of powerful people exerts influence over a public institution. I have been discouraged witnessing the refusal to change. Universities often tout their social justice commitments as part of their brand. It is ironic as they are hostile environments for marginalized students. There is also little tangible action on issues of inclusion and transformation.

However, powerful stakeholders do not entirely control the culture of a university. That culture is made up of all of us who move through it every day. And we all participate in its competitive, individualistic practices. Sometimes, it seems like we have no choice. Class privilege relies on such competition. Within its bounds, some individuals succeed at the expense of others. Misogyny, racism, and homophobia, for instance, occur between workers in a competitive market. We must challenge these things in classrooms and the workplace. Otherwise, silence maintains hierarchy and violence. Whether silence results from investment in privilege or fear of reprisal, the effect is the same.

In this book, I'm interested in how class, gender, and labor are lived in the university. I'm interested in how these inequalities shape higher education. At a more local level, I'm interested in how these inequalities sabotage our voices. Each concept of my title has its own chapter. The first chapter is about class. In that chapter, I explore class inequality and union experiences. These experiences reveal that education is experienced differently based on class. The second chapter is about gender, more specifically misogyny. I share my difficult experiences to show men are still privileged in the academy. This is despite claims of post-feminism in the US. The third chapter is about labor. I look at labor through the concept of burnout. It helps us see all the things demanded of us in the institution. But it also shows where our work ethics sabotage us. The final chapter is about finding a voice. I review some of the barriers I established in the earlier chapters. I identify the healing potential of an intellectual community as a strength of the university. In my conclusion, I recommend changes to universities based on my experiences.

My work does not exhaust every possible experience within the university. That is not my aim. Instead, I hope that you, the reader, tell your own story. I want you to foster relationships with your peers, colleagues, teachers, and friends. Complain, build an organizing campaign, and create spaces of rest and thoughtfulness. We do not have to fight our battles alone. So this book is from me to you: in solidarity.

1
Class, unions, and contesting the status quo

"I just don't see the problem," the administrator said. She was a well-known faculty member. "We are not bound by the union contract."

"Yes, you are," I told the administrator. "You have to pay workers the set rate. You have to pay them on time when the work is complete. This is wage theft."

She scoffed. "I can't believe we have to deal with something this ridiculous."

I took a deep breath to disguise my disgust and impatience. Years of customer service work helped me hide my feelings.

It wasn't surprising the faculty member thought this was ridiculous. She had tenure, a very large house, relative fame, and, oh, a good salary. She hailed from a class position where wage theft would probably never happen to her.

I didn't say anything. I waited for the silence to get awkward. The accountant of the department spoke up. He asked for records of the students' hourly work.

This case was a difficult one to work on. It exposed the institution's reliance on unpaid student labor. It also showed a lack of care. It was surprising. This, from a department interested in improving the university! The department could drag its feet on reimbursement. They could wait until the student graduated. Or they could wait until the student dropped the case. After all, this professor's wages weren't missing. She was only mildly inconvenienced by this process. Our grievance was an attempt to redress an institutional wrong. But she acted as if it were a personal attack. And perhaps it was personal for her. One faculty's success came at one student's expense. She benefited from this, if indirectly. Our union grievance refused this logic. We challenged the class inequality of the student-faculty relationship. No faculty member's comfort should require a student's impoverishment. Her expressed, classed disdain for speaking about money implied we were being uncouth. Such an attitude created a middle-class taboo. One should never speak about money in public.

In this chapter, I discuss class within the university. I am interested in how some succeed at the expense of others. First, I define the relationship between class and education. Then, I consider middle-class attitudes and behaviors. I briefly discuss my class background in this section. (I'll return to it in the third chapter.) This helps illustrate some assumptions of class and education. These assumptions interfere with students' ability to get their education. To conclude, I describe unions as alternative spaces within the university. I analyze a union grievance to demonstrate avenues for change. I put our struggles as workers in the context of other unions around the world.

Defining class and education

Education occupies a fraught position in the reproduction of class. Education bears some of our heaviest ideologies about improvement and social mobility. We treat education as a cure-all for class inequality. We often look to it for bootstrap stories. Poor kid comes to university, and leaves successful! Getting a college degree has become a necessity for social mobility. The paths for other kinds of life have narrowed.

Education cannot deliver on these promises for everyone. This is because class is a relation. Class operates as a zero-sum logic. Put another way, capitalism distributes resources according to scarcity. One person's success means another person's deprivation. Rather than a personal failing, the system only allows for success or wealth for a limited number. The logic goes like this: there isn't enough for everyone. That could be money, time, food, shelter, or even education. But this is artificial scarcity. Within this system, resources tend to go to those who already have them. The privileged have the means (money) to secure those resources, depriving others of their basic needs. We create things as a society that we do not need. We prefer to enrich the lives of those who are already rich. (A good example is a personal jet.) Education cannot counter this structure entirely. It is one way to secure a place within the hierarchy. In the social mobility story, there are only a few spaces to rise to.

One feature of class is, obviously, money. Class is whether you have money or don't have money. Money can include property or assets that provide a safety net for hard times. For example, say all graduate students in a department make $20,000. That figure means different things for everyone in the department. Some have generational wealth, parental assistance, or other kinds of security. Some have children or crushing debt. In another example, we could look at a university president's salary. She makes hundreds of thousands of dollars (if not more) and owns her home outright. She might be paid less than other university presidents who are men. But she occupies a position of power in the hierarchy. Her salary is dependent on the undergraduate student working a minimum-wage job. (We could do this same example with sports coaches. The inequality is even worse.)

Another aspect of class is whether you control someone else's labor. You might even control your own. A distinction has long been made between the working class and the owners of the means of production. But it's useful to break that down further. Supervisors and teachers, for example, are also workers. They have power over their students (who are or will be workers). Within this dynamic, we see abuse take place. I began with the example of wage theft. This inequality also creates sexual harassment and sexual assault. A male faculty member can threaten a student with a grade or a letter of recommendation. Privilege means you can control others' labor, including sexual labor. Demanding sex in return for a grade is an abuse of power. In this case, both class power and male privilege.

Class inequality is visible in ideology. Usually, it is the ideology of those occupying power. This is a complicated point. Ideology is how we think about our relation to something. In an unequal society like the US, that other perspective distorts our thinking. For example, I was a student of literature. I learned great literature is difficult, esoteric, and not political. Later, some teachers challenged this apolitical reading. But still, literature's politics were difficult, sneaky, and removed from daily life. In other words, literature wasn't something you could **use**. This is a specific, classed vision of literature. It reflects a professional investment in literature as the domain of the privileged. (And here we mean college-educated and wealthy.) It also reflects an investment in one's own position as an interpreter. Such a vision was alienating for me. My relation to literature was broken for a long time because of this education. I felt that, given my background, I could never write. I could never join the ranks of writers. In this brokenness, inequality gets rewritten. I took on the perspective of the field. This field was not created by or for people like me.

My example may be specific to literature. However, each field has its ideologies that relate to inequality. We could also restate "ideology" as "stories we tell ourselves". These stories are sometimes less about truth than about surviving. Let's put it in monetary terms. You are a student. You need a letter of recommendation to earn a fellowship. You need a faculty member to support your career. You have to get to know them for the letter. So you take on their interests and style, ensuring they'll recommend you. This is identification, part of that distortion of perspective I discussed above. Your perspective comes to align with a more powerful person's. Identification, in this case, comes from a place of disempowerment. But the story we tell is that this dynamic is "professionalization". You hope for success by becoming like this other person. You hold onto this hope no matter the pain it causes. This is a stripping away of self.

There are more or less healthy versions of identification. In my example, I'm focusing on its negative aspects. It reproduces inequality by protecting those with privilege. It remakes us into what the powerful need. It makes us adopt their perspective instead of our own. I saw many students defend their advisors against accusations of bad behavior. They did so because they were dependent on that faculty member. They defended them because they wanted the same privilege the faculty had. They did not want to rock the boat and risk losing that privilege. A relation of dependence exerts a force on us. It compels loyalty and immunizes cruel or abusive behavior. Especially as the student may have little control over their situation. We can apply this thinking to different situations like family, politics, and other workplaces.

Class is also evident in our narratives about education. In our stories about education, we can see the threads of identification and wealth. In the US, we treat education as a path (if not *the* path) to individual and social betterment. We don't ignore obstacles to education. Instead, we celebrate the individual who overcomes them. Obstacles include social isolation, poverty, poorly funded public schools, and rising tuition costs at universities. (There are recently popular memoirs about such upward mobility. I will not cite them because I think they're unhelpful.) We participate in class-based ideology when we describe college as a balm for inequality. We ignore that social mobility reveals inequality. It doesn't challenge it. It points to both the impoverished situation and the more ideal one. The individual is responsible for making that journey. Instead of expanding the social safety net, we tell individuals to go get an education. This is not a solution to capitalism or class inequality. It's a way to maintain it.

To say education is a path to a better life is sort of true. It is truer for some than for others. But this truism ignores other motives for education. College is more than job training or a social mobility tool. We reduce our ideas of who we want to be when we accept these narratives. As a result, many students choose majors based on money. I had many conversations with students getting their education for others. They had to please their parents. They had to get a good job. Education was not a way to become themselves. Thus, students go into different forms of study based on funding and promises of work. When we apply market values to education, we adopt the ruling class perspective. Economic thinking precludes visions of education as empowerment or self-discovery. Many assume working-class kids, in particular, select their majors based on money. Often, we do not. Transfer students from community colleges are more likely to choose humanities degrees than their wealthier peers.

In this section, I discussed several aspects of class. I analyzed money, control over labor, and ideology. In the next section, I apply these concepts to my classed experience of education. I discuss all three aspects of class: money, labor, and ideas about education. I describe how inequality manifests in our relationships within the university.

My class story

Class shapes the trajectory of one's life and education. We refuse to see this in America, mostly because we refuse to see class. In this section, I want to talk about my educational journey. I share my personal experience to illustrate the abstract concepts from the last section. It also provides context for the following chapters.

My experience of social mobility has been uneven. In 2010, I got my acceptance letter to college; I didn't know anything about the university. I just knew I wanted to attend. For years, going to college had been my goal. With that letter in my hand, I felt immense pride. My parents did too. I was the first person to go off to college. I was the first to live in a dorm! To support me, my parents took out a burdensome loan. This kindness offset loans I would eventually accumulate. Even with scholarships and going to an in-state, public university, I ended up accumulating about $40,000 worth of loans (this was from both my bachelor's and my master's). I was lucky to be at a state school with low tuition. I also had some scholarships.

When I first got to school, I did not settle on a major right away. I floated between criminology and journalism. I worried about a career and making money, but I disliked my journalism classes, and I wasn't sure I wanted to work in the criminal justice system. An economic rationale made me miserable, so I became an English major. I loved literature. I wanted to write. I thought it would be the most enjoyable way to get a degree. I knew I could make money as I had previously, in customer service. Picking a major based on making money made no sense. I didn't need to learn how to work more. Instead, an English degree would help me develop parts of my life that had nothing to do with work. My desire for education, then, was less about economic gain than personal growth.

My experience of college got less and less enjoyable. English literature was no longer a subject to pass the time, no longer a way to ponder the world. As a master's student, it was something I studied to pay the bills. I started as a teacher's assistant in large non-major courses, making $8,000 a year (no health insurance). The next year, I made $12,000 (still no health insurance). By the time I got to my Ph.D., I was making $24,000 a year (with health insurance, finally). My relationship with literature became less free. It became a way for me to climb the social ladder. I moved on to the next degree because it was a way to make money. I had no idea what I wanted to research (or even how to research, really). I just knew I wanted to be in the university.

I achieved levels of education no one in my family had. However, graduate students occupy a strange class position. We work at lower wages and with less autonomy than faculty. The work I did as a graduate student was not like a professor's. I didn't have control over assignments or the direction of the course. I could sometimes assign texts I enjoyed, but I couldn't design a course from scratch. I only taught a true literature class once, and someone else designed it. I left teaching to become a sexual harassment prevention trainer. Even this job had little room for creativity. My job was the same: train (or teach) as many people as possible. The university certainly got its money's worth.

In addition to the workload, I found the social environment alienating. My peers made frequent references to status. They mentioned their parents' wealth, their private education, and their access to opportunities. They spoke in abstract language that was alien to me. They held opinions that made no sense (until I reckoned with their class position). They often used these things to put others down and signal their own worth. I was surprised by the attention-seeking and need for validation. I didn't want to participate in this. I didn't know how. For a long time, I stayed silent and withheld from social interaction. But then, I began to speak like my peers. I deformed myself to fit in. I became good at what they did. When I spoke, I did not speak to other people; I spoke to valorize myself. I espoused opinions I did not believe just to fit in. I pretended to know more than I did. I never asked for help. I hid behind these classed protocols.

In performing this identification, I became like my peers—except I was different from them. My working-class background meant I had a different view of the world. I had different expectations about friendship and education. I worked part-time or odd jobs constantly. I had debts to pay and costs to cover. While I could perform some social aspects of class, its material gains were elusive. Unlike my peers, I couldn't find jobs that aligned with my interests. I didn't know how. I went back to customer service work. It was what I knew and what I knew how to get.

There was one social practice I never could perform: a particular identification with faculty. One silly practice in many departments is calling professors by their first names. Since we were graduate students, we were allowed to do so. Undergraduates, lowly beings that they are, were not allowed to do this (I'm being sarcastic here). They had to show respect. But I found it a useful distancing tool. To say "Dr. X" meant recognizing differences in power. Calling professors by their first names erased that difference. It caused significant pain for my colleagues. They were sometimes rudely reminded that their identification emerged from their subordination. One student tried to convince her supervisor that she too had expertise in their field. The professor swiftly and cruelly put her down. Other students were surprised to be sexually harassed by a professor who had seemed so cool.

The hierarchical nature of the university means we act out of self-preservation rather than solidarity or community spirit. I found this attitude alienating. A mentor once told me we had to play it safe as she was working with senior colleagues. From her perspective, she had a career on the line. My position as a student made me less important. This was difficult for me. It meant I had no solidarity with the faculty (or perhaps, they had no solidarity with me). Everyone looked out for themselves. I witnessed this need to protect and propagate privilege so many times I don't even know where to start.

An example: in a theory course, a professor held up a thick stack of papers. Then she said, "Look what you've given me this semester." I was horrified. She had stolen our discussion and thoughts for her next book (this is a kind of plagiarism). I was so angry I spoke to my classmates about what she had done. Unfortunately, they did not see things the way I did. My peers told me it was a reasonable price to pay. She was a brilliant professor, they said, and they wanted to study with her. Their response shocked me. Did it occur to them that her "brilliance" may have belonged to her former students? Wasn't it ridiculous that this happened in a course about social justice? We have yet another example of class difference: the person whose work relies on the impoverishment of others. In this case, it was a theft of ideas rather than wages.

Hierarchy transforms us. We prefer to believe we can inhabit the institution unchanged. Nick Mitchell argues that, because of class differences, tenured faculty in social justice fields are not in solidarity with their students. They may share other marginalized identities with their students, but for most, their solidarities lie with themselves and their property. This means they enact class power within and outside the university. Their solidarity with the ruling class might be implicit, but it is solidarity nonetheless. As students, we learn ways of being from our faculty. This is how we learn (in part) self-involved commitment to the preservation of status. We, too, become bound by unconscious solidarities that reify class power rather than interrupt it. I cite this example here to show that there are challenges in creating solidarity, even among people who consider themselves politically aware. I never filed a grievance over the professor's theft. I assumed no one in the department would support my case.

Despite all this, I achieved my doctorate. Unlike some of my peers, I did not follow the middle-class arc of achievement. I did not land a tenured professor position, a lucrative private position, or launch a young and brilliant writing career. The normal interpretation is that I did not try hard enough. If I had worked harder, then I could have had these things. Such an analysis assumes all students are equal. We might believe they are—I do believe this—but there are material differences between students. As I've mentioned, some students have wealthy parents. Some may have gotten private schooling. Some received mentoring and resources they needed from a department without difficulty. And they didn't have to work part-time jobs, so they could dedicate themselves to unpaid professional development. Some had resources to achieve those positions which require considerable risk. A tenure-track position can take years of adjuncting and fellowships to achieve—not everyone can afford this.

I did not have the luxury of seeking a tenure-track position because of different limitations. During school, I didn't have time for networking and conferences. I also struggled with how to ask for help. I didn't know what good mentoring looked like. I didn't know what faculty could help with. I sometimes barely got my reading and writing done. And I certainly didn't have time to perfect my craft. I worked multiple jobs and had other responsibilities. I had to secure a job as soon as my PhD ended. I had bills to pay. Time and money were stretched thin. I couldn't afford to play the lengthy job application game. Instead, I took an available salaried staff job at a university. I started at a pay grade far lower than my peers. I also had to finish my dissertation while I was working. My job was not close to what I wanted to do (write and study literature). I watched my peers take on more opportunities and achieve more visible success. (Carolyn Kay Steedman points to envy as one of the more unattractive class feelings.)

After my doctorate, I feel that my life hasn't significantly changed. Bills are still worrisome. Writing is still a small corner of my life. I still work odd jobs. While I gained important skills, the material change in my life is minimal. I say this not to denigrate my experience. After all, I have refused to apply economic logic to parts of my life. That is a choice I continue to make despite its downsides. Rather, I am making a point about what an education is for. I am still subject to our cultural expectations about education. I reject the narrative that education should only be for improvement or mobility. I want education to mean different things in life. That could be a better sense of color, as Oscar Wilde wrote, or a deeper sense of self. But I can't entirely shake the sense that my life was somehow supposed to get materially better, as if by magic. This cultural wishful thinking takes the place of sustained political effort.

That's why, in the next section, I want to move away from my personal experience. At an individual level, not much change happens. Instead, I want to show how collective struggle can change the landscape of education. I look at how unions target class power on behalf of students and student workers. Unions work to improve worker autonomy and working conditions. They can create an environment where we can work and receive our education free from harm. These battles are key if we want to remake the university.

Organizing for power

"You shouldn't have to be independently wealthy to get an education!"

My organizing mentor spoke passionately into the megaphone. This was my favorite slogan. We were writing a different story about education. Education, we argued, should be affordable for everyone. We argued that students should be adequately paid for their work. We opposed unfair treatment of students based on their identity. We also refused to treat education as solely an economic prospect. Together, as workers, we demanded accountability and material redistribution from the university to the workers it relied on. Our union understood education as a place for individual and collective self-determination. We worked to realize this every day. It wasn't a far-off goal we just talked about.

I talk about my union experience in this chapter because it is part of my class story. My dad was a steward in his union at an automotive plant in Michigan, where I grew up. Unions were directly responsible for my parents' ability to provide for us as kids. Unions, then, were familiar to me. They were a place to bond over shared experiences of work. In this section, I describe what a union is and how it challenges class inequality in the university. I provide a specific example from my organizing experience.

I loved being in my union. Whether I was rank-and-file or a steward, I felt like I belonged. Being in a union requires us to recognize what we have in common with others. It requires seeing how problems are numerous and connected. If we don't have something in common with our fellow workers, we learn how to be in solidarity with them. We work with them to craft demands. We listen to stories of injustice. We address the wrong they are drawing our attention to. (An injury to one is an injury to all—another of my favorite slogans.) Union organizing requires developing political skills like power analysis, one-on-one conversations, listening, and critical thinking.

Our union included academic student workers (teaching assistants, research assistants, recitation leaders) and postdoctoral scholars. We were all committed to changing the landscape of higher education to be more accessible to everyone. While I eventually walked away from union work, I treasured my time working within it. I felt like I belonged in the union. I felt lonely in my department but not in the union. My focus on problem-solving was valued in my union. My union emphasized solidarity and community. This is a working-class ethos. It is anathema among most academics. The academy is driven by a middle-class commitment to self-interest. (I once had to listen to a professor ridicule solidarity as the province of idiots who hadn't read Foucault—direct quote.)

So how does a union work? We have short and long timelines. First, the long timeline. Every three years, we renegotiated our union contract. These are the protections and benefits that workers negotiate for beyond the bare minimum. It includes things like limits on hours worked, pay raises, health insurance, and discrimination protections. There are a lot of items in a union contract. These are just a few. When we worked on an organizing campaign for a new contract, we had to talk to members. We had to find out what they needed and what challenges they faced. Once we identified those challenges, we crafted them into demands. One year, we demanded a sexual harassment prevention program, building on the energy of #MeToo. Another year, we demanded gender-neutral bathrooms, working with our queer students.

Every cycle, the process was the same. After we had our demands, we pressured university leadership. We needed them to meet our demands. University leadership, though, did not want to meet them. Why? They didn't want to give raises, pay for health insurance, or provide childcare. It costs money. And they didn't want to spend money on labor. Such spending interferes with other, extraneous spending. Further, our demands empowered workers. Empowered workers don't come cheap and they don't submit to abuse. This makes a workplace less efficient and profitable for employers.

To get our demands met, we had to try different strategies. Here as some examples of tactics we used. Once, we occupied a board of governors meeting. Additionally, we wrote op-eds about student workers being rent-burdened. We also went on strike with a majority vote. Picketing the university showed the community what the university was doing. It also showed leadership we were serious. This was all a lot of work—not just the endless hours calling members. We also had to organize the strike, coordinate and occupy the meeting, and write the op-eds. We were still fulfilling our jobs as students! Those with comfortable class positions do not have to engage in this kind of exhausting advocacy. Their comfort and privilege are already built into the system. They don't have to fight for it.

Of course, the board of governors and the president don't want to change anything about the university: it suits them to pay student workers little, to ignore harassment, and to refuse to pay health insurance premiums. They will continue bringing in their large salaries. The university will continue to churn out workers good at following instructions. In the end, we were able to win major improvements for all our members. Our pressure campaign worked for a variety of reasons. Universities don't like bad press. They also don't like the disruption posed by a strike. In the end, we got most of our demands.

This kind of large-scale organizing happens in the community, too. In 2020, we allied with Black Lives Matter organizers. We worked with other unions to remove the police department from the labor board. Using our unique position, we were able to further the goals of both our members and community organizers. We all lived in the same city and wanted to be safe. The police department failed to reform. Despite promises to improve, they continued using violence. These promises had happened with the last round of Black Lives Matter protests around 2014. Our union led the call to remove the police department because of this failure. We participated in protests. We did our usual one-on-one organizing. We succeeded in removing the police union from the labor board. This opened up new campaigns for deciding how to fund community safety.

I mention this campaign because unions matter in many ways. They are significant for the workers they represent. And they are significant for the community they belong to. Unions have the power to organize at many levels, coordinating struggles. In the next section, I'll analyze a more local organizing campaign. I demonstrate what organizing to change a departmental culture can look like.

Organizing within departments: The demand letter

Unions can transform department cultures. These kinds of campaigns can spread across a university, too. If one department makes changes, other departments feel they can (or must) follow suit. In this section, I talk about a campaign I worked on to gain more support for students. I also discuss challenges to department climate. Climate refers to discriminatory attitudes, whether explicit or implicit. Campus climate is as much a part of our working conditions as wages.

I worked on a campaign for a department that was struggling with poor funding, nonexistent mentorship, and racism. The students in this department were under a lot of stress. As a result of COVID-19, they hadn't met their colleagues in person. There was uncertainty about funding. The department also refused to change deadlines despite the pandemic. This created a general feeling of isolation, especially among first years.

A student came to me with their distress. I helped recruit her colleagues for a group conversation. To do so, she had one-on-one conversations with her colleagues, who then had one-on-one conversations with others. These one-on-one conversations are a vital tool for organizing. They entail talking to those in our lives about problems they have. Then we help get them involved in a project to make changes. As a result of these conversations, almost all of the department's first-year graduate students showed up to the meeting. They had ideas and experiences to share about what was wrong. They had ideas about how to improve the department. They were willing to work together to change things. We decided to put pressure on the department by writing a collective letter.

The collective letter lists demands. It also contains the signatures of everyone participating in a campaign. This list shows leadership a few things. First, there is a significant group of unhappy people. Second, this unhappy group of people is willing to cause trouble. Finally, it shows leadership that negotiating is in their best interest. Letter writing is difficult. You have to consider all members' issues and personalities. There are disagreements about demands. Sometimes there were clashes of personal and political style. There can also be discomfort with signing the letter.

During final revisions, a black first-year student emailed the group. They wrote to the whole group. They were disappointed that the letter ignored black students' experiences. Specifically, we left out explicit racism in the department. I felt disappointed that this student felt unwelcome, but I was glad they spoke up.

I thanked them for telling us about their difficult experience. At our next round of revision, we let the student talk as we took notes. We learned a good deal about racism, especially on the part of a well-known professor. We discovered serious inequalities and a celebrity culture. Celebrity culture is when faculty are revered for their intellectual work and their harmful behavior is ignored.

We had not known about the specific intersection of racism and celebrity culture in the department beforehand. We added demands about training for racism and a prohibition on racial slurs in the classroom. These demands deepened the letter to the department by registering the variety of indignities that students experienced. It also let the department know what their students were experiencing. We pointed out poor funding, precarity, uncertainty around their degree requirements in light of COVID, racial slurs in the classroom, and a lack of faculty of color mentors for students.

The point of a union is to gain dignity at work for workers: that meant tackling all of these things. We submitted the letter to the department chair, the unit chair, and advisers. This began a long series of meetings. We secured more funding for students. We also convinced them to change exam requirements because of the pandemic. We disagreed on the faculty support for students. The department maintained this support was not a problem. They failed to hear that students felt isolated and professionally adrift. Professional development in the department was unevenly distributed. Some students stood a better chance of working in their chosen fields than others because of this lack of care. We didn't convince them to implement professional development measures. Equally, they never addressed the racism that we disclosed in our letter. That professor was never held accountable. The department rejected our demand for diversity education for faculty.

We don't win everything at once. But we had to keep organizing. To keep up our momentum, I organized a solidarity letter from other graduate students. These graduate students expressed support by signing a letter that backed the students' demands. It also expressed sympathy for their situation. Seeing all the signatures on the letter was a huge boost in confidence for us. Others saw their struggle and supported what they were doing. The letter communicated to department leadership that they were being watched. This is particularly helpful. I think, most of the time, leadership wants to help students, even if just to make themselves look good. This desire to look good was, I think, worked powerfully in the students' favor.

The campaign fizzled from a lack of direction and from distraction. The lack of direction had to do with how we were going to push the department on issues like racism and professional development. They had refused to budge. What tools did we have at our disposal? We never got around to answering this question because of a significant distraction. One student tanked the campaign by making it about their personal experience. Unfortunately, this student's experience wasn't discussed during our letter campaign. The student had not been present. They weren't interested in working with us to develop particular demands. Instead, they took over meetings with leadership. They complained, at length, about their experience. This meant the whole hour went by without addressing a single demand.

I tried to intervene. The student felt their right to speak was more important than our campaign. I was not supported in my confrontation with the student.

It was a disappointing end to a campaign. What I am describing is fairly common, though. Individualistic and competitive tendencies destroy a campaign's solidarity. Stonewalling from the administration is another way to end a campaign. Sometimes, we do achieve success. In this case, the success was partial and opened the doors to more organizing in the future. I hope this story shows you the benefits of organizing. We can redirect resources to students. We can also learn how to support each other in our different struggles. The department ultimately did not feel responsible for the students. But we created a wonderful community that, last I heard, was still advocating for themselves.

In the next section, I connect our union struggles with an international context. Union organizing within education is happening all over the world. We have a lot to learn from other struggles, but we can also see patterns across our experience. From these patterns, we can form solidarity with others.

International context and conclusion

Under capitalism, education is a means to create a stratified workforce. Some have access to education and others do not. Within the educational system, students have different outcomes. Because of this inequality, worker solidarity is vital. Often, we are divided from other workers, especially on college campuses. We are invested in individual advancement. We believe in myths of self-sufficiency. We are often separated from those who belong to a different class. We have to let these attachments go and find connections that may be difficult to make. We have to throw our lot in with others. Organizing means creating solidarity, local and international. It's hard work. Bringing these smaller struggles into a bigger fight can transform all education, not just universities.

In this section, I briefly detail other countries' educational battles to provide context for the conditions in the US. In educational systems abroad, workers face similar conditions. Education is under-resourced, removed from democratic control, and stratified by class. But there are significant differences to be aware of. In comparing these situations, I hope to spark connections.

In England and Australia, unions protested austerity measures. Austerity measures were economic cuts to government programs and budgets across the board. This was supposed to cope with the international financial crisis in 2008. Austerity measures happen instead of increasing taxation on the rich. They shift the burden of economic crises onto working people. So, within education, these measures cut teacher salaries and increased class sizes. There is less financial assistance to students, as well. These measures enrich and empower a select few at the expense of everyone else. Similar cuts to social spending appeared in many countries, including the US.

There are other examples of local struggles we can learn from. Teacher strikes in West Africa have made similar demands for improved salaries and better learning conditions. Nigeria recently had teacher strikes to improve university research capacities. This improvement could help its universities' international presence.

The Global North unfairly dictates research and commands most of the funding. For African universities, this has meant their degrees are less desirable to the market and their students struggle to find work. In European countries like Hungary, teachers have struggled against the nationalist curriculum. This curriculum does not foster critical thinking and contributes to authoritarian power. It instills an unquestioning belief in government and its version of history. In France (as in the US), the education system is segmented by class where students from working-class backgrounds do not have access to the same quality of education as their wealthier peers.

But there are other countries where teachers are well-paid and highly respected. Some examples include Finland, Japan, and South Korea. However, in Japan and South Korea, teachers and students suffer significantly from burnout and social pressure. Many other universities also suffer from a lack of academic freedom. In places such as China or Indonesia, for example, scholars are under intense scrutiny to produce acceptable scholarship. This includes scholarship that avoids certain topics under the penalty of law. We do not have a similarly dire situation in the US. However, we can notice that some topics are frequently attacked. Ethnic studies, for instance, were banned in Arizona. Professors have been fired for their political opinions, too. I point out these different situations because any struggle over education has to tackle local problems. That does not mean we can't identify common ground.

In this chapter, I discussed how class operates within the university. I argued that unions could challenge that. In the first section,

I discussed how money, class trajectory, and stories about education obscure institutional failures. These institutional failures are also social failures. We, as a society, seem to think only a select few deserve good lives. In the second and third sections, I looked at how unions contest inequality through organizing. Finally, I considered struggles in universities around the world to illustrate the wide range of changes needed. These examples can serve as models for activists elsewhere. (I also hope that it connects us with those activists. We have a lot to learn from them.) In the next chapter, I continue analyzing the way competition shapes university environments. This time, I turn my attention to gender and misogyny.

Discussion questions

1. What aspects of student life do you feel are unfair? Where have you struggled in school that frustrates you? If you haven't struggled or don't see anything unfair, why might that be?

2. What do you think the value of education is? What stories about education did you hear growing up?

3. What are your perceptions of unions? Have you or someone you know ever been in one? How does this affect how you feel about them?

4. How would you narrate your educational journey? How has your class background affected it?

5. With a partner, practice a one-on-one conversation. Get to know each other and your struggles as a student. Do you have anything in common? What differences can you identify between your experiences?

Recommended further reading

Chu, A. L. (2018). I worked with Avital Ronnell. I believe her accuser. Chronicle of Higher Education, August 30, 2018. Available at: https://www.chronicle.com/article/i-worked-with-avital-ron ell-i-believe-her-accuser/ [Accessed 7 June 2021].

Cruz, C. (2021). *The Melancholia of Class: A Manifesto for the Working Class*. Repeater Books.

Fire with Fire. (2020). An Introduction to 1-on-1 organizing conversations. *Fire with Fire* blog, April 2020. Available at: https://firew ithfire.blog/2020/04/19/an-introduction-to-1-on-1-organizing-conversations/ [Accessed 28 July 2024].

Giffel, K. and Postal, C. (2020). Crisis pedagogy. *Reimagining the PhD*. Simpson Center for the Humanities, 22 June 2020. Available at: https://simpsoncenter.org/article/crisis-pedagogy [Accessed 26 April 2022].

Gutiérrez y Muhs, G., Niemann, Y. F., Gonzalez, C. G. and Harris, A. P. (2012). *Presumed Incompetent: The Intersections of Race and Class for Women in Academia*. Utah State University Press.

Mitchell, N. (2019). Summertime Selves (On Professionalization). *New Inquiry*, October 4, 2019. Available at: https://thenewinqu iry.com/summertime-selves-on-professionalization/ [Accessed 7 June 2021].

Mitchell, N. (2020). The View from Nowhere: On Frank Wilderson's Afropressism. *Spectre*, pp. 110–122.

Steedman, C. K. (1987). *Landscape for a Good Woman: A Story of Two Lives*. Routledge.

2
Misogyny, sexism, and knowledge production

I have been in many classes when only men spoke. I have been in classes when teachers only responded to male students. I have been in university spaces where men shout women down. I witnessed survivors of sexual assault being told that their experiences don't matter because the attacker deserves their education. (The attacker, in this verbal abuse, is always a man.) I watched those same survivors drop out of school. I was told my experiences didn't matter. My harasser deserved to be in the department too. In a grievance meeting, a white male professor's right to use a racial slur was upheld. The discomfort and pain of the black women who brought the complaint were dismissed. I have been in university spaces where men undermined, trashed, and vilified women. Their crime? They disagreed with a man (who was, by the way, wrong). Sometimes that woman was me. I and others have been treated as secretaries by male graduate students. After all, they generate ideas and women write them down. I witnessed a sexual assault victim drop out of school because she couldn't get help. Her attacker was a faculty member. Once,

I had to intervene in a classroom argument. A male student said women were overreacting to a short story about domestic violence. Men aren't all bad, he said. A female student shouted back, but all women suffer from them.

These stories are just some examples of how misogyny shapes our learning environments. We come to learn as students. We stay as faculty to create scholarship and teach. We work as staff to improve the experience of the university. Misogyny and sexism make all of these tasks difficult. Misogyny and sexism interfere with work, study, and developing one's career or one's voice. Misogyny is both a form of inequality and a way to maintain it. Misogyny and sexism create a hostile environment for women. As a result, it becomes difficult for women to stay in the university. Male privilege may be unevenly held in the academy, but it remains a default setting. And women pay for it.

In this chapter, I focus on sexism and misogyny in higher education. I detail experiences of harassment that reveal a misogynist social context. First, I define sexism and misogyny, focusing on sexual harassment as a common form of misogyny. Then, I turn to its adverse effects, on women's mental health and their careers. I discuss the specific effects misogyny can have on knowledge production. In the conclusion, I consider feminist accounts of misogyny from other countries. In doing so, I hope to demonstrate the reach and impact of misogyny.

Defining sexism and misogyny

I'm in a meeting of graduate students. A white man held forth on the inadequacies of a female professor. She had the audacity to give him a 3.9 instead of a 4.0.

"What a bitch," he said.

There was total silence in the room. The majority of us were women.

A friend reminded me of this incident. We were discussing our shared misery related to this man. He asked me if I remembered flinching when the man said the word "bitch." I shook my head, taken aback. He said, "I'll never forget that you flinched."

For my part, I'll never forget that I stayed silent. I think I was shocked. But I also recognized something. I saw that this place of prestige was as misogynistic as anywhere else in my life. In this section, I'm going to discuss what misogyny and sexism are. Class is not the only form of inequality that the university produces. Indeed, misogyny and sexism can be part of class inequality. They affect women's place within the labor market. I start my analysis by close reading the initial anecdote. Then I define misogyny and sexism in the university. I focus on sexual harassment in this section as one illustration of the hostile environment.

Let's return to the anecdote I started with. I like its simplicity: it reflects everyone's participation in misogyny. We have a seemingly minor incident. A man calls a woman a bitch. Her crime? Not giving him the grade he wanted. The grade he felt entitled to. The man is a student, and the woman is a professor. The professor certainly occupied a position of privilege relative to us. She had power over grades, wealth, and tenure. None of us said anything in that professor's defense. And that silence implicated every woman in the room. Despite being the majority, we weren't empowered to challenge his privilege. None of us prevented his tirade. Entitlement and anger in his voice suggested he related this way to other women. (I did not see this at the time.)

Misogyny and sexism, as Kate Manne has argued, are ways of keeping women down. Sexism can be found in explicit and implicit rules or ideas about what women can or cannot do. At one university, a professor published a sexist rant on his blog. He said that women were bad at computer science because they weren't biologically suited to it. This is sexism. It is an idea about women based on a false narrative of women's inferiority. Misogyny is less about ideas. Misogyny attacks women directly, using a variety of tactics to silence or discredit them. Misogyny rises to meet women when they transgress male privilege or some other social hierarchy. Misogyny, then, could be sexual harassment, or sexual assault, of a woman within a computer science department. Both would put her down in the context of a male-dominated department. So we have the difference between an idea and an action. In both cases, individuals enact misogyny and sexism but the problem is not reducible to an individual idea or behavior. They are social actions enabled by a hostile environment. They reproduce that hostile environment.

Misogyny and sexism shape our social spaces. They determine who deserves care and support, who deserves freedom, and who belongs. Women, of course, experience misogyny and sexism differently. But, within the university, all move through a historically male space (as well as white and wealthy, among other modifiers). Misogyny and sexism maintain male privilege over a space. That privilege includes entitlement to women's labor but also entitlement to social goods. For example, tenure-track positions overwhelmingly go to men. As do those positions' wealth, prestige, and social visibility. Men receive more care, in general. This isn't true for all men because of different forms of inequality.

But relative to women in their social group, they still receive more social care. Men's social comfort is upheld at a cost to women.

Sexual harassment is a common form of misogyny in the university. It creates a hostile working environment for women based on sex or gender. It includes things like unwanted sexual comments or requests for sexual favors. It can also include diminishing remarks about women or feminism in general. It is misogyny because it targets women in a man's world, the university. Universities treat sexual harassment as a neutral phenomenon. The solution, from the university's perspective, is more education. But such a solution ignores the real power differences between men and women. It also ignores the institution's failures to support women at all. Sara Ahmed documents how difficult and unreliable reporting harm is in a university, especially when it is related to sexual violence of any kind. Women are often doubted. The perpetrator's privilege, especially if it's a man, is typically upheld. It doesn't matter whether he's a student or a professor.

Abuses of power are enabled by a lack of accountability. They are also enabled by a social context that devalues women. Unequal pay, for instance, ensures that women occupy more precarious positions than men. It also literally communicates that they and their labor are worth less. The social hierarchy of a university also produces misogyny. As we saw in the last chapter, those with privilege wield it over others. And we know this is true in the case of sexual harassment. Undergraduate and graduate students tend to be harassed by their more privileged peers (usually men). For postdoctoral scholars, they tend to be harassed by faculty. And for faculty, they may experience harassment from other faculty.

Any teacher can be harassed by a student. The power dynamics are complicated, but women experience this often. (As I once experienced.) The differences in power make people reluctant to speak out. Even if the victim has some privilege, it's too risky. There is little solidarity among women in a university. And this isn't just my opinion. Troy Vattese notes studies that observe a lack of political consciousness among women, especially faculty, within the university. Such consciousness is too costly.

As a result, many women leave the academy because of hostile work and study environments. This hostility partially explains the low rate of women in the academy and their high rates of turnover. Women leave academia at higher rates than men, whether they are faculty, staff, or graduate students. Only 27 percent of faculty at four-year institutions are women. At a faculty level, women do not receive tenure at the same rates. Misogyny, in any of its forms, also causes significant distress. This means lost work time, papers not written, dissertations not finished, lives ruined. It means someone came to the university full of dreams and is forced to leave, if only by attrition. Their social world tells them, over and over, **you are not important**. They are acceptable collateral in the university's daily operations.

One way to measure the frequency of sexual harassment is through a campus climate survey. This type of survey asks questions about different forms of discrimination and helps us understand, beyond official reporting, the experiences people are having. In one climate survey, which I worked on as a researcher, 2,500 academic student employees were surveyed. Of those, 2,355 respondents answered questions about harassment. Of that group, 33 percent had experienced harassment and

32 percent had witnessed it. While harassment was experienced across different identity categories, the total hovered around 30 percent for most groups. Forty percent of women (both cis and trans) experienced some form of harassment, and 62 percent of nonbinary and agender students reported experiencing harassment. Additionally, many respondents selected "I don't know", which could indicate that they witnessed or experienced harassment but either did not find a corresponding description in the survey or did not wish to disclose it.

Most respondents did not admit to being harassed directly. The questionnaire asks, "Have you experienced sexual harassment?" Many, if not most respondents, answer no. When faced with an abstract concept like that, it can be hard to think. So we also asked respondents about concrete behaviors. We asked about whether they experienced or witnessed comments belittling women. We asked about derogatory comments about feminism, which also indicates a hostile environment. We also asked about unwanted sexual advances (someone asking them out on a date) or touch and uncomfortable conversations about sex. Based on these questions, many people experienced harassment. It is valuable to focus on specific actions rather than the broad category of "harassment." Even I had a hard time applying "harassment" to my experience!

Harassment is enabled by other factors. Harassment is strongly correlated to experiences of isolation (experienced by 45 percent of the total). It is also correlated with poor mentorship (22 percent) and career uncertainty (55 percent). Further, almost 60 percent of students in the survey were rent-burdened. That means they don't make a livable income. Harassment, then, is also a class dynamic, insofar as it affects workers and their working conditions. Such conditions curtail students' self-determination. Think back to the demand letter from the last chapter. The students demanded more faculty of color to counter poor mentorship and career uncertainty. The organizing work we did was about preventing harassment at its root.

This survey emerged as a strategy after #MeToo organizing in the academy. My job as a sexual harassment prevention educator was also a result of #MeToo energy. Despite this, the lack of progress around harassment and sexual assault endures. There may be discourse about these things, like articles or essays that suggest we talk about them all the time. But at a local level, survivors often do not disclose, and, when they do, these conversations are difficult because of a lack of options. Within the university, two major factors for silence are fear of retaliation and a lack of institutional trust. There are protections against retaliation through Title IX and union contracts. (Our union had the most progressive retaliation protections in the country.) These reassurances do not inspire confidence in those who need to report. Title IX offices, historically, have not significantly improved the environment for women. Many who come forward feel betrayed by the institution because of unhelpful Title IX investigators. A vicious feedback loop repeats itself. The university remains a patriarchal space.

In this section, I have explained misogyny and sexism with examples. I have also defined sexual harassment as a kind of misogyny. I showed the prevalence of sexual harassment as a problem. In the next section, I consider what effect misogyny has on knowledge production. A university does many things. It doesn't only produce research. Research, however, is one of its distinguishing qualities. It is a major part of its identity as an institution. So, in the next section, I investigate it as a site of inequality.

The consequences of misogyny

It was a cold, sunny day. I stood by the Puget Sound, crying into the phone. I told my friend, C, about what was happening to me. I described the constant texts and emails, the avoidance of my office, the bullying and belittling. I shared her how I couldn't cope. There was a moment of silence. She said, "Kaelie, it's okay to be upset. You're being harassed." Her words shocked me. I stopped crying. Harassed. How had I not seen it? It was my job to recognize and teach others to recognize harassment. C said, "Having a job about harassment doesn't mean it can't happen to you." She added that it's hard to see what's going on when you're in the thick of things.

I just kept telling her the details. He belittled me in front of others. He diminished my attempts at writing. He said my interest in feminism was racist and harmful. (I later learned he targeted women of color in other departments.) Once, he proposed we collaborate on a project. He narrated his idea to me and then asked if I could type it up and get the documents ready for submission? I had to have it to him by a certain time. I participated in his misogyny directed at a friend and fellow organizer. He vilified and belittled her, and I did not defend her. I took my harasser's side and protected his privilege. It all just kept happening. I was overwhelmed and paralyzed by what was going on. I was afraid to think or speak up. I let this man take over everything, giving up my voice and freedom.

(A relevant story: Months before I told C, I tried to tell another colleague. Her response was hostile. She told me critiquing a white man was boring and white feminism. All I had done was tell her about his harassing behaviors.)

In this section, I use my experience to demonstrate how misogyny shapes knowledge production, both in content and in publication. This experience changed my trajectory as a graduate student. It changed what I wrote my dissertation about and the style in which I wrote. I learned, as an organizer, to help others tell their stories. I politicized other people's experiences and organized campaigns around them. However, I did not treat my own experiences with the same seriousness and care. I'll return to knowledge production in my final chapter. For now, I focus on the aspects relevant to my harassment experience.

After my conversation with C, I collected stories of harassment and misogyny. I read stacks of novels, finding examples of misogyny that mirrored my life or revealed new aspects to me. It was difficult work: I cried a lot. (I still do.) I was heartbroken for the women in the stories, but it was also consoling. I wasn't crazy. Misogyny was real. I scrapped my original dissertation idea. I was going to finish my Ph.D.; I was not going to drop out. I was not going to go silently. Too many had left because of this horrible place. I wanted to leave a testament to the harms of the institution. If it demanded a dissertation from me, it would get a long story about how miserable it made me.

To write my dissertation, I had to overcome my doubts about feminism. As a graduate student, the only thing I learned about feminism was that it was outdated. I couldn't get too attached to it as a result. Doing so was evidence of my political failures. (I don't think any other social movement is spoken of like this.) Some argued it was (a) the province of white women and (b) women were already equal to men. Neither of these things is true. For one thing, feminism is a vibrant and contentious history of women arguing. They argued over what a better world looks like and how to understand patriarchy. For another, women are **abstractly** equal to men. And I consider myself equal to any man. But this ignores the very real ways women are disempowered relative to men. Women face the same kinds of subordination feminists theorized in the 1960s— history doesn't move that quickly. Sexual assault and sexual harassment shape our educational lives. Misogyny diminishes our voices. Sexism shapes the labor market, keeping us in some jobs and out of others.

Another difficulty in overcoming my doubt was access to knowledge. Universities have historically been the domain of wealthy white men. I've made this point before. This means research and the organization of knowledge reflect their interests and experiences. Thus, one form of inequality is not having access to the knowledge you need. I had to research misogyny extensively on my own. This is evidence of oppression. It was vital knowledge that was not part of any curriculum. This, alongside the earlier judgments about feminism I mentioned, made me feel like feminism wasn't a subject worth writing about. It made me feel like my experiences were trivial. I was fortunate to take a feminist theory course with my advisor, but even that course was stuck at a level of abstraction that made it difficult for me to apply it as a thinker.

Being told that feminism is passé or too corrupt to use is harmful. This narrative pervades both the university and organizing spaces. Rarely is feminism treated as having a history of thought worth studying and wrestling with. Such a narrative makes it difficult to apply feminism in daily life. It is also part of the unique misogyny of the university. It makes it impossible to point out the obvious. It feels ridiculous to say: men are privileged, and women are diminished. The world simply responds, **yeah, who cares**? I eventually learned not to care about this apathy. I wrote it all down anyway. I didn't care what people thought about my writing. I was angry. I was angry that my dissertation was born out of necessity rather than choice. I was angry that I felt so alone. I was angry at myself for my own misogyny. I was angry that no one had ever spoken up for me like they had for him. And when he had done harm!

Chanda Prescod-Weinstein's book *The Disordered Cosmos* documents a similar experience in her development as a scholar. As a black agender woman in physics, she was sexually assaulted by a colleague in her field. In addition to her experiences of racism within the university, this experience of sexual assault affected her style of writing and style of thinking. Movingly, she describes the time she loses to flare-ups of post-traumatic stress disorder (PTSD). She struggles for days with equations or presentations that would take her assaulter a minimal amount of time to complete. After seeing him at a conference, she has to recover from the shock for a long time. This emotional aspect is often discounted when we talk about the relationship between misogyny and knowledge production. While Prescod-Weinstein does not name her attacker, it is still brave for her to write about her experience. I have struggled for a long time about whether to write my own experiences at all.

Like Prescod-Weinstein, my voice was a response to misogyny. But this ended up being a double-edged sword. Denouncing misogyny placed me in the position of complaint. It made my voice legible in ways that diminished it. After all, the time I spent denouncing harm was time not spent writing about other things. Further, for some readers, I was immediately dismissed. My problems were not big enough. My concerns were too localized. My voice was too annoying. Misogyny, after all, wasn't seen as a major issue from a broader perspective. Women are constructed as annoying and angry by patriarchy. This is how others can refuse to hear us when we speak up about suffering. Feminism, in this way, is about having a community that can hear you and do your voice justice. It can also mean discounting yourself in the eyes of those who view feminism as marginal or dangerous.

I turned to feminism as a way to cope with my social isolation. Feminism helped me feel the love and connection I did not feel at that time in my life. I needed it to help me with the harm I experienced. I turned to women writers because I didn't have anyone else to turn to. Writing my way into feminism meant writing my way out of a marketable dissertation, at least if I wanted to stay in the academy. No one was looking for the type of personal feminist literary criticism I produced. Nonetheless, my dissertation elicited deeply personal reactions from readers. My stories upset some readers, not because they would rather not hear them, but because they responded with their own experiences of harm and unhappiness. They, too, felt unsupported in departments. They felt like they had nowhere to turn for help.

Even if my dissertation was afield of the current academic conversation, it had some value for individual readers. That seemed like enough.

Eventually, I left my department because I couldn't cope. I reduced my social circle to a few people I saw alone, off campus. I avoided group gatherings. I didn't attend my graduation. I am not alone in my departure. But I never felt lonelier than I did as I left everything behind. After I left, a friend told me that my harasser had targeted a woman of color in another department. This was after I had absented myself. I thought about how lonely she must have been. I thought about how lonely I was. I thought about how no one had helped either of us.

Feminist education: Harassment prevention

My situation had been deteriorating for a while. Then the pandemic intervened. Upshot: I did not have to see my harasser. While this did not prevent the constant emailing and texting, it was a relief. Around the same time, I also got a new job. I became a sexual harassment prevention educator. I joined a small team of women. Our job was to educate union members about sexual harassment. Our workshop taught bystander intervention, reporting options, and union protections. In this section, I want to explain how this education worked. It demonstrates how we might contest misogyny through education and organizing. In the last section, I felt isolated and overwhelmed. But the work I did as a harassment prevention educator gave me comfort. It also kept me in the university until I finished my degree. Even though it eventually contributed to my burnout, I loved my time on that team.

Universities treat education as the solution to everything. It is not. For example, education is seen as the solution to sexual assault and sexual harassment on college campuses. Consent education is considered a gold standard in the prevention field. People treat it as a cure-all for sexual assault. This completely ignores the facts. Abuse of power lies at the heart of sexual assault and sexual harassment. It stems from inequality. In general, universities do not address misogyny as a collective problem. We treat misogyny and sexism on a case-by-case basis. We measure whether it's "that bad." We treat individual men as the source of the problem. At the same time, we refuse to hold any men accountable at all! Further, we ignore the social structure that enables and perpetuates it. I say "we" here because I have been in the violence prevention field for a while. And I have witnessed all of this. Education, ultimately, takes the place of consequences for abusers and empowerment for survivors. We are fine with women and other survivors bearing all the consequences. (Excuse me while I scream into the void.)

Even though education alone cannot solve the inequality we are facing, I loved the work I did as a sexual harassment prevention educator. It was unique compared to the more harmful kinds of education I delivered in my career. Our work was feminist for several reasons. First, it focused on power and hierarchy. We accounted for different levels of power at the level of identity and the level of structure. Second, we emphasized organizing as one way to prevent sexual harassment. Most education about sexual harassment makes the individual responsible for not getting harassed. Or it requires them to learn a different language for consent. (The implication here is that lack of vocabulary causes assault.) Instead, our training built a community to contest the causes of sexual harassment in the first place. We did not blame the victims.

To help our participants, we engaged in power analysis. We analyzed the different social settings of a department. We also looked at different forms of power. For example, lab settings operate differently from classrooms. Students often work in labs at odd hours. They might be alone. And they are under their hiring instructor's power. This might be because of grant funding or because they are co-authoring a paper. Working with students on problems they faced every day, we found places to organize students for change. One grievance that came out of organizing included a researcher misgendering a student in their lab. This counted as gender harassment. We learned of this because that student attended our workshop. They learned the steps they needed to take to rectify the situation. They also saw they had a supportive community behind their report.

Tailoring this education is vital. While harassment may happen in all departments, the way to fight will change based on context. This depends on who is involved and how. For example, teaching a group of English Ph.D. students about power inequality in the lab is not helpful. It might help them learn about their peers. It does not help them learn the inequalities and harms of their particular department. Learning how to analyze our environment to see who has power and how they are using it is crucial. For a group of English Ph.D.s, we might talk about the "theory boys" phenomenon. "Theory boys," as a mentor called them, use progressive theory to put down women (among others) and perform their own genius. They take up a lot of space in classes as well. (Yes, this is a thing! They're the worst.)

When organizing for change, analysis is the first step. But it has to be followed by action. In our curriculum, we also taught bystander intervention skills. Alongside this, we taught participants how to recognize harassment where it appeared. We also practiced how to intervene. We talked about what might be hard about it. I know that intervening is difficult. It took me years of teaching these trainings before I learned how to interrupt problematic situations and feel safe and confident doing so. Practicing, giving advice, and discussing with my co-trainer taught me how. I wished I had had this education—this community—earlier.

A final story, this time about how this education had a real effect. I was facilitating a Zoom meeting of about 300 union members with another steward. We had a tight schedule and no room for discussion that day. This had been decided by leadership. I had to apologize when people raised their hands. We simply had no time. At one point, my co-facilitator interrupted me. He said, "Well, I want to hear what people have to say, so we're going to take comments." He decided to undo our agenda and rules because he felt like it. He implied I was a censorious bitch keeping the people down. He undermined my authority as a facilitator of the meeting. Even worse, he interrupted because one particular student wanted to speak up. And that student was a well-known misogynist in another humanities department. (Perhaps every department has at least one.) We had heard many complaints about this guy. I still had to hand him the metaphorical mic.

Both of these men proceeded to berate leadership's lack of radical vision. They claimed to be in touch with what membership wanted. (Keep in mind neither of these people were adequate organizers.) I was annoyed throughout this whole process. I had other things to do. I thought both of these guys were a waste of time. But my body was still shutting down: I was shaking and angry. When the Zoom ended, I slammed my laptop shut. I burst into tears. This time, I knew what was happening as it was unfolding. I still felt powerless to stop it. I played the polite, white feminine role to a tee. I acted as if nothing were wrong.

There was something different about this moment, though. It was class and male privilege and a dash of misogyny, sure. When I was being interrupted, younger women from my department were posting in the chat. They sent messages of support and encouragement for everyone to see. They were using micro-affirmations, one of the skills we teach in our workshops. This is a way to send small messages of affirmation. You're sending love to those in your social spaces, making sure they are seen. Micro-affirmations create feelings of belonging and social cohesion. For several weeks after the event, many women reached out to me. They said they were sorry for how I was treated in the meeting. Never before had an experience like this been acknowledged. It was also a direct result of my prevention work. All the supportive messages came from participants in my harassment prevention workshops.

That moment of support from my department peers meant the world to me. I felt my work mattered and that I mattered, too. For a moment, I also felt less alone. For countless hours, I spent time with others treating sexual harassment as a real political problem.

It wasn't just a silly feminist idea, as it was treated elsewhere. In this section, I discussed sexual harassment prevention as a tool against misogyny. I detailed what that education can look like, emphasizing education about power and organizing for change. And then I provided an example of how I witnessed the effects of such an education. To conclude, I consider how misogyny affects women's education and voices in other countries.

Misogyny abroad and conclusion

Misogyny is a transnational problem. This means that women's experiences of misogyny are connected, but we must learn to make those connections. Unfortunately, most research on sexual harassment focuses on American universities. It is also unfortunate that most research on misogyny focuses on sexual harassment. Misogyny is a problem with many manifestations. Because academic research is not often translated, I turned to novels to learn about universities in other countries. I recommend Cho Nam-Joo's *Kim Jiyoung, Born 1982* (South Korea), Meena Kandasamy's *When I Hit You: The Portrait of the Writer as a Young Wife* (India), Kang Hwagil's *Another Person* (South Korea), and Bernardine Evaristo's *Girl, Woman, Other* (England).

All these novels investigate the challenges women face in universities (and beyond). Women struggle against misogyny, racism, pressure to marry, loss of voice, and blatant preference for men and protection of their comfort. These novels broaden our understanding of misogyny and account for other pressures women face. These authors show misogyny experienced at the hands of spouses, boyfriends, fellow students, and friends. In Kandasamy's work, the narrator is married to a professor who beats and assaults her. He is protected by everyone around them. Her book draws attention to the specific expectations Indian women face in marriage and how progressive politics does not preclude misogyny. (The book is a great example of "theory boys" gone wrong.) In Cho's novel, female students are excluded from job fair activities. The departments claim they are less desirable to the company. Women are also driven from their jobs by harassment in hostile environments.

The extreme competitiveness of South Korean universities is a unique feature, but the fact that women experience sexual assault is not. Kang's work builds on this vision of the disastrous consequences of competition. In Kang's novel, feminism is non-existent in a university where women are complicit in each other's abuse. Kang also shows the differences in privilege between female faculty and students. It is a damning portrait. Evaristo's novel is sensitive to the class dynamic in England. One story in her novel depicts a young Anglo-Nigerian woman with immigrant parents who uses university to both build her career and make a good marriage. She survives an extreme assault that drives her to be ever more successful, all the while managing her trauma alone.

There are journalistic accounts of recent feminist activism that can help us here, too. Hawon Jung's book, *Flowers of Fire*, is about the feminist movement in South Korea. She documents the #MeToo movement within schools at all levels. The abuse of students was enabled by the control teachers are allowed to exert over their students. Teachers are highly respected in South Korea, making holding them accountable difficult. But young women in South Korea put up a terrific fight, publicizing the abuse and being disruptive. They are a great example we can learn from. Leta Hong Fincher, in *Betraying Big Brother*, writes about the feminist movement in China. Her work gives us a sense of the stakes of misogyny. In 2015, women protesting sexual harassment in public spaces were arrested and interrogated by the Chinese government. Their families were threatened. The government treated these women as threats to the government's narratives about gender in China. We can see here that misogyny is an issue of the state and international influence. Controlling women, in the Chinese context, for instance, is seen as central to building a national economy. The government wants to maintain an image of patriarchal power to counteract the West.

A final example: In South Korea and Japan, women receive college educations at a high rate. But they face barriers in finding work. This is because of explicit preferences for male candidates (as mentioned in Cho's novel). There are also large gaps in wages as well as sexist expectations around motherhood. Women are expected to resign when they have a child. Employers assume women will not be around for long. Motherhood is a given. Within the university, preference for men has a direct effect on whether women are mentored. It also affects whether they are given the resources they need to succeed as students and workers. Fighting for your well-being and right to participate can have dire consequences. Fincher's book, as I mentioned, describes state retaliation and censorship of protests over sexual harassment.

All these books show forms of misogyny that call for unique forms of organizing. (I especially recommend Fincher and Jung for learning about feminist organizing.) But they also point to some key features that remain the same. Isolation is a common feature of all these women's experiences. Interestingly, none of the novels feature feminist organizing or any real feminist community. (Evaristo's book is a collection of women's points of view but isn't in itself a feminist community.) Precarious class positions are also common. Kandasamy's narrator loses access to money and is not allowed to work. All of Kang's characters are working-class women. Evaristo's account focuses on one young black woman's class mobility after sexual assault arising from race and class-based disempowerment. Struggles with voice also appear in almost all the works. Kandasamy's narrator can no longer write. Kim Jiyoung starts speaking in dead women's voices. (All these women were her friends, killed, directly or indirectly, because of misogyny.) I was also struck by the way violence warped women's sense of time. It takes time to respond to and recover from violence. And that directly interferes with other endeavors. Finally, the preference for men creates inequality of resources. Put simply, women get less of everything and are expected to be happy with what they do get.

Feminism remains vital and central to transforming the university and the world. We live in a context where most people assume that progress is linear. Many think feminism is no longer important. We can see from all of these examples how feminism is desperately needed. What is also needed is connecting with feminists elsewhere in the world. The consolidation of male privilege is very real. We saw that universities are vital to economies and state-building. Thus it matters that, within them, women are subordinated and attacked. The university is not an island. It reflects the culture it is a part of. Through its social relations and its means of knowledge production, it reproduces that very same culture. It is our job to intervene in it.

In this chapter, I showed how misogyny shapes women's experience of education. They experience subordination, divisions of labor (where men get the more prized work), and isolation. Misogyny enables men to maintain control and privilege over a space simply by making it unlivable. I've also shown that this dynamic interacts with class. I concluded by looking at how organizing and education could contest misogyny. I examined other universities to see what we might learn from other contexts. In the next chapter, I further explore the interaction of class and gender through my experience of burnout. This burnout was a direct result of the divisions of labor within the university and my experiences of misogyny.

Discussion questions

1. Have you experienced or witnessed misogyny? Did this chapter help you name any experiences you have had?

2. How would you have reacted in the situations of misogyny I've described? List your answers from the most realistic to the most ideal. We all think we are straight talkers with courage, but sometimes reality gets the better of us.

3. Practice micro-affirmations. In class, if someone speaks up about an idea and you like it, say so out loud! In a social club, give a compliment to someone to get to know them better. Micro-affirmations can be used in any space but are especially helpful in a place like the university.

4. **Scenario:** You are in a classroom where one student, a man, keeps answering all the questions the professor asks,

without giving anyone else a chance to speak. What would you do?

5. **Scenario:** Your friend has started to miss class and you're concerned about her mental health. She tells you about being bullied by someone in class. What would you do?

Recommended reading

Note: Any of the novels mentioned in "International Context" are highly recommended!

Ahmed, S. (2021). *Complaint!* Duke University Press.

Ahmed, S. (2019). "On Complaint." YouTube. Available at: https://www.youtube.com/watch?v=4j_BwPJoPTE

American Association of University Women. (2024) Fast Facts: Women Working in Academia. Available at: https://www.aauw.org/resources/article/fast-facts-academia/ [Accessed 14 April 2024].

Empowering Prevention and Inclusive Community. (2021). "Equity Survey." Available at: https://www.washington.edu/safecampus/epic-program/

Giffel, K. (2024). "A #MeToo Novel That Must Be Read #WithYou." *Public Books*, 13 February 2024. Available at: https://www.publicbooks.org/a-metoo-novel-that-must-be-read-withyou/

Manne, K. (2017). *Down Girl: The Logic of Misogyny.* Oxford University Press.

Prescod-Weinstein, C. (2021). *The Disordered Cosmos: A Journey into Dark Matter, Spacetime, and Dreams Deferred.* Bold Type Books.

Vattese, T. (2019). "Sexism in the academy: Women's narrowing path to tenure." *N+1*, issue 34. Available at: https://www.nplusonemag.com/issue-34/essays/sexism-in-the-academy/ [Accessed 13 Mar 2024].

3
Burnout, class, and academic labor

The summer of 2019 was my favorite time in graduate school. I was studying for my comprehensive exams. I sat in my apartment all day, reading and taking notes. My partner dragged me out of the house on Saturdays, mostly to make sure I still knew how to walk. Otherwise, I was reading. I immersed myself in a long list of books I had chosen to study for my exams. I studied modernism, the history of the novel through women's writing, and feminist theory. Having so much time to myself was unreal. All I did was read and study. I could feel myself unspooling out in time. The stress of my exams was real—I did not want to fail. But I often forgot about the exams in the thick of my reading. It was such a luxurious experience. I wanted to build my whole life, my whole identity around it.

Turns out, most of academic life is not like this.

It looked a little more like this:

Spend two hours spinning around one paragraph in Chapter One; push your body through high-intensity interval training; attend a grievance meeting with an administrator who screams at you that her racist training is not racist; agree to more union committee work because no one else is going to do it, and you want the organizer to think you are capable and a good leader; doubt your ability to lead anything but your own destruction; start a second page for the to-do list; spend one hour editing a three-sentence email to your dissertation chair, combing for tone and competency, and making sure you don't sound too needy; spend another hour trying to decipher the subtext of the reply email and any advice it might contain for surviving your days, even though you don't understand the basics of what she's suggested; spend three hours in meetings, managing your affect and others'; run three trainings on sexual harassment in one day, and nearly collapse from exhaustion; delete an email from a harasser; cry for an hour, feeling drained, gross, and powerless; berate yourself for the difficulty and anguish; reassure yourself that there are people who thrive here, so just toughen up and act like them, you're fine; keep doing this day after day, week after week.

Tell no one.

When I wrote that paragraph, a few years ago, I was burnt out. I worked long days, and then other days, I couldn't work at all. I wasn't sleeping. I was arguing with my partner. Panic consumed me. Some days, I would cry before I started a training session. My internal narrative was one of self-violence. I couldn't believe how ridiculous I was being. I thought I just couldn't hack it. I wasn't good enough to be in the university. I couldn't take so much work. I couldn't endure its social misery. It wasn't until I started writing my dissertation that I saw this narrative for what it was.

Eventually, my ability to work was nothing compared to the massive nature of the institution. My ideals as an organizer and feminist conflicted with the institution. Cases kept coming in. There were thousands of people to educate. The institution changed not one ounce. In retrospect, I'm sure our educational efforts made a difference for those who attended. There were cases of grievances emerging from these trainings, as participants would come to us with their problems. This was a definite sign of change. But I could no longer see these positives; I just saw an unremitting future of harm and tedium. I had to remove myself from all this work just to think about what was happening.

As I started writing, I found I wasn't alone in my struggles. Burnout was a phrase that I didn't know until suddenly I heard it everywhere. It was a concept that helped me see my problems all at once: too much work, struggling with harassment, and feeling lost as a doctoral student. Burnout is a useful way to think about education and institutional harm. It draws into focus the gendered divisions of labor that unfairly burden women. It lets us look closer at classed ideas about education and the implicit protocols that leave many students behind. Burnout helps us see assumptions about deservingness and support within the institution.

In this chapter, I discuss my experience of burnout to illustrate overwhelming working conditions. I begin by defining burnout and labor. Then, I discuss different sources of burnout as they relate to class and the work ethic. I also assess the role of gender in my work ethic. I consider practices within the university that contest burnout. Then I turn to an international discussion about burnout that is not limited to the university. My analysis points to serious discontent with work, especially among educated workers.

Defining burnout and labor

Once, I complained about how miserable the university made me. A faculty member asked, "Is the university different from any other workplace?" It was a fair question and one I've spent a lot of time thinking about. Few other workplaces have narratives about their public benefits and their commitments to diversity. When I worked at a restaurant, for instance, I was never confused about the significance of my work. No one ever told me it was a privilege to be making low wages and getting sexually harassed. At the university, it was the exact opposite. I was alienated by the gap between the university's narratives and what I witnessed every day.

In this section, I define burnout as a political feeling. It expresses dissatisfaction with how we organize and distribute work. Often, discussions of burnout blame the individual worker and their habits. In this section, I want to turn away from this individualistic focus. So, in addition to defining burnout, I'll also discuss labor. We aren't individually responsible for our line of work or its conditions. Even if we have unions to contest both of these things, we are not free from overwork or unhappiness at work. Labor is socially organized and helps us see broader, systemic failures that cause worker burnout (among other problems).

Burnout, as a word, is a bit overused. Because of this, it can be difficult to define. It has a clinical meaning, but it also has a common-sense meaning. Clinically, burnout is defined as exhaustion, an inability to keep doing your job. Its hallmarks include cynicism and ineffectiveness. It typically applies to those in professions like social work and nursing. More recently, other workers have started to use it. The causes of burnout are multiple. Stress from work contributes to burnout, as does overwork. The overwork, though, has a particular ideological character.

For instance, I worked more as a younger woman. Especially in high school, I had a job and school and did care work at home. In college, too, I had a full-time class load and worked every day at the restaurant while maintaining a social life. I did not live exhaustion in the same way I did as a graduate student. My life was not as stressful. In graduate school, I worked from five in the morning until seven, sometimes nine o'clock at night. I moved from dissertation to training to organizing all in one day. I still somehow had to be a spouse and dog parent. I had to be a friend. I also had to maintain a fellowship with my friend C. We had to dedicate a certain number of hours every week to our project.

The situation worsened when the pandemic arrived in March 2020. My workload moved online and accelerated beyond my control. My life was reduced to my 398-square-foot apartment. My partner's job security was in question. Our relationship itself was tense. Amid the stress of the pandemic, my union had more organizing to do. I had to rewrite the training curriculum at work, making our workshops suitable for Zoom. I had no idea how to write my dissertation. I was struggling with the harassment and isolation I described in the last chapter. I wasn't sleeping because I was working constantly. Then I lay in bed with anxiety and stress. The only solution to feeling terrible was to do what I knew best: work.

Burnout isn't just about quantity, then. It refers to a crisis caused by a gap between our ideals and our work. Many people work more than 40 hours a week without experiencing burnout. Burnout is about both labor and our ideas about that labor. We live with a common narrative to "do what you love." We also live with narratives about social change being our personal responsibility. In other words, we have to love our work. And we have to dedicate ourselves to social change. What makes these ideas harmful is that the work available is dictated by the market, not by human needs. Further, we are dedicating ourselves to social change in an unequal social world. Most of the time that feels like banging your head against the wall. Other times it feels like being gaslit.

I felt like I had to work to compensate for the university's failures. All my work, organizing, and research railed against the wrongs of the university. This was a profoundly alienating experience. I felt I had to make a seamless whole out of my life and work. I had to perform a kind of political subjectivity that was wearing me out. And I felt I had to perform that simply because the institution caused so much harm. The more I tried to hold everything together, the more I fell apart. There was simply no pleasure or sustenance in my life. I didn't feel like I should have any pleasure.

But where do these ideals come from? To whom do they belong? More importantly, who do they benefit? It benefits employers for workers to be emotionally connected to their jobs. You don't have to pay as much if a worker is driven by a higher mission. Sometimes it is admirable to forgo high-paying careers. Mostly, those careers dedicated to helping others are poorly paid. Such careers are gendered and racialized as well, in that certain kinds of people are funneled into them. Social work careers are a good example here, as is nursing. My work as a sexual harassment prevention educator was gendered. I went into it because of my experiences with and research about the subject. I went into it because it aligned with my political ideals. I felt my job reflected something of who I was. For a while, I enjoyed that.

I believed deeply in my union organizing and my harassment prevention work. I believed in it in a way I did not believe in my research. It was work I felt comfortable doing. It seemed to make a difference. I didn't feel out of my depth or out of place. That sense of ease meant I pushed myself hard. I saw the struggles of my fellow students and felt I had to work harder to ease those struggles. I thought that working harder would somehow change things. It doesn't. As I continued working without rest, I started to lose it. I hated the world. I wasn't able to schedule workshops effectively. I wasn't writing my dissertation either. I started skipping organizing meetings. I avoided people. I thought everything was terrible. Other people were bad, I was bad, and my project was bad. I needed to torch everything.

Defining ourselves through labor is one cause of burnout. This is a classed phenomenon. Scholar Erin Cech has documented the harm of both narratives I've mentioned. The "love what you do" narrative, in particular, deepens class inequalities. Only some people can afford to do what they love, and they are, typically, wealthier than others. Working-class kids in the university usually end up further afield of their preferred work. So, we find another cause of dissatisfaction with our work arrangements. I cite Cech here to underscore the value of class histories for understanding sources of burnout. To truly understand one's class position, especially with regard to work, we have to look at our class histories. Where we sit at a given moment is not reflective of our overall class trajectory. Nor does it show the kinds of stories about work we grew up with. I'll discuss this more in the next section.

At its most simple, labor is about who does what for whom and who benefits from it. Benefits can be wages, profit, or emotional and social capital. Class, gender, and race can describe kinds of labor and compensation. Labor is also a way to understand how class, race, and gender are embodied. They are not just ideas. Within the university, gendered and racial disparities within the faculty body are one example. Then you have the disparities between faculty and students and those who work in food and custodial positions. Even within a group, like, say, graduate students, you have divisions of labor. These divisions are gendered and racialized. Some get better lab tasks than others. Some get fellowships while others do not. Some perform work less related to their degree just to get by. Labor, then, differentiates between who gets desirable tasks at various levels.

Labor also includes the work we have to do just to belong. I have been talking about various forms of inequality thus far, including class and gender. I have also pointed to my struggles to fit in and feel like I belong. The work I do to make myself smaller, more acceptable, is also labor. This labor of fitting in or survival has been called "ontological labor" by Ruthanne Crapo Kim, Ann J. Cahill, and Melissa Jacquart. I cite their concept because I found it so eye-opening that I had to include it here. It refers to all the work we have to do to fit in, socially. This is on top of more obvious forms of work like delivering a lecture. So, for example, think of a black woman giving a lecture. She has to manage her presence to ensure her audience respects and listens to her. This could include pitching her voice higher to seem less threatening.

She may dress in a more professional way than her peers. She may have to avoid telling students directly they are wrong. Other forms of ontological labor could include coping with trauma as a result of harassment or assault, correcting someone when they misgender you, or reporting harassment. It also appears in forms of perfectionism. This is a feeling that you have to be better than everyone else just to get by. Being unable to ask for help is another example. These are all responses to inequality. Ontological labor demonstrates how labor is unequally distributed within the university. Thus some workers feel more pressure around their work.

Turning to labor in this way means we have to ask a few questions. One, what is our relationship to work and where did it come from? What place do we think work has in our lives? Do we have a sense of self-worth beyond work? Additionally, does our laboring benefit us or others? How does our social context cause burnout? In the next section, I discuss my personal history to answer some of these questions.

Class and our work ethics

A friend and I organized an MLA panel about first-generation PhD students a few years ago. We wanted to know what university was like for first-generation PhDs. This is a larger group than you might think. It includes first-generation students and students with the highest degree of education in their families. It was a generative conversation, full of energy. I was surprised when 100 people attended! Many people shared stories of difficulty but also stories of triumph. Many expressed that they wished they'd had more help from their departments. One comment, in particular, stood out to me. A faculty panelist observed that one graduate student seemed to do a lot of non-degree-related work. This is in addition to working a job outside the university. The panelist observed that, for working-class students, the university could be a particularly difficult place. The university would, he argued, take advantage of our willingness to work. It relied on our survival-based work ethic.

In the depths of my burnout, I thought about this comment a lot. And I think he's right. If there's one thing I know how to do, it is work. But there were many things the university required that I did not know how to do. I didn't know how to network or plan for a career a decade in advance. I was lost on how to write long research papers, and how to develop theories and ideas. (The reason I was drawn to novels as a doctoral candidate is that they're illustrative. They give me something concrete to work with. I struggled with theoretical abstraction.) But I thought working hard would make up for what I didn't know. I ended up turning toward things I **did** know how to do.

Identification with work is a key part of my class history. A good work ethic was one thing my parents instilled in me. Like my parents, my labor, myself, was all I had to sell. Watching my parents struggle with money and work shaped my attitudes about work. They had five kids to raise. Working-class writers Carolyn Kay Steedman and Cynthia Cruz document the working-class girl's unique relation to work. It is how she redeems the struggle of her parents. I didn't want to experience the suffering they did. I also wanted to heal their struggle through my hard work. This is also gendered in that I was instilled with a desire to be "good," something inflicted on girls. Through labor, I would be made good. I would become good.

Our work ethics develop long before we enter the university. I witnessed my parents struggle with their jobs. I saw my mother walk out of a job that treated her poorly. I saw my dad work night shifts at the manufacturing plant. He would then juggle childcare while my mom went to work or attended a night class. Hard work was the only option. It got you through crisis after crisis, if only for a little while. When I was younger, we lived close to family and so there were zones of life that had real joy. Not everything was absorbed in work, but as I grew older, this kind of community fell apart. We moved away; relationships were difficult to sustain. At that point, I had to help my parents as much as I could. I cared for my siblings until I moved out, but it was never enough to fully ease their struggles. I was always referred to as a good helper, a phrase no one ever used to describe my brother. It meant that I was good both at paid work and at caring for others.

My attitudes about work are not entirely conscious or rational but have proven durable. Internalized compulsions to work are a form of violence. They limit us to our capacity for labor when we are so much more. We internalize these attitudes to survive. But work and labor aren't just our ideas about them. They are material actions carried out in the world. Labor is a means of survival. Because of this, labor becomes a central part of the self, especially when all you have to sell is that self. I felt this deeply, and it would come to affect how I did my work. Labor became a means for me to get the attention and love I thought I had to work to earn. (Incidentally, men do not have to earn affection.) I barrel through crushing amounts of work simply because there is no alternative. My work echoes the way my parents moved from one state to the next, chasing jobs they needed to put food on the table. There is no room for "I don't want to," or even "I'm tired," only room for "just do it." Bills need to be paid. This kind of thinking is disastrous. On the one hand, I have to work hard to achieve the security my parents also sought. On the other, I desire a life worth living. I want a life in which one has fulfilling relationships and an autonomous sense of self. A self that is more than the work she performs.

My working ethos was, then, developed at a young age, way before I got to the university. But, as I have shown throughout this book, there are uniquely toxic aspects of the university. Many aspects of my work tapped into my constitution as the "good child" and "good daughter," and now, "good woman." I use these phrases ironically. Being a good woman means laboring for others at the expense of yourself. It means suffering in silence. Being good is an imperative that women must meet. We are expected to be morally and aesthetically good, with no room for failure. This meant more ontological labor for me. I had to perform the "ontological labor" of playing nice with frequent misogyny. I had to hide my stress and anxiety from harassment. I had to work harder than everyone else with few resources for help. Further, I had to make sure I didn't upset anyone around me. (It makes me laugh and cry that men can harass with impunity, but one misstep will have a woman belittled *at least*.) And just to reach a basic level of knowledge and competence that I, as a working-class kid, did not have.

My orientation toward labor benefits the institution or any other employer I might have. They can get a considerable amount of work from me with little pay. I am largely a self-governing worker. (Which you learn, of course, in graduate school.) I posed little challenge to the way of working the university demanded. I was eager to succeed, no matter what. I did not challenge (on my behalf, at least) the toxicity of the culture. Being a good worker, after all, means not making waves or causing issues. Being a good woman means the same thing.

No wonder I was burned out by the end.

Healing from burnout

Curiously, the solution to burnout in every single book I've read on the subject is contemplation. It means a cessation of work in favor of thinking or rest. It is a way to come back to yourself, your preferences, and your better nature. Perhaps it is not so curious—all the books were written by (former) academics, so it makes sense they would prize their calling as a means to healing. Anne Helen Petersen sums it up best when she writes, "The burnout condition is more than just addiction to work. It's an alienation from self, and from desire. If you subtract your ability to work, who are you? Is there still a self left to excavate?" In this section, I detail how I recovered from burnout. I look at my experiences of writing and contemplation, which helped me wrestle with my constitution as a woman and a worker in the university.

I came to the university to write a dissertation, but it felt closed off to me. While I was struggling with all my tasks, I watched colleagues bypass all the struggle or it seemed like they did. They shut themselves up in their offices, produced articles or papers for a class that stretched to a hundred pages, and refused certain kinds of labor to focus on their writing. They seemed to have no guilt about focusing on their writing. I resented this: why couldn't I do that? They also seemed to have a belief in their work and vision that I had never had. I couldn't give up all my organizing and educating, I thought, it would make me a terrible person. My mentor eventually said to me, "You are going to have to give something up". This upset me because I knew she was right. But it would be tantamount to admitting failure.

Retreating from public life is often the first step to recovery from burnout. This is the story of thinkers like Jonathan Malesic and Zena Hitz. Malesic left a tenured faculty position because of burnout. He discussed how his ideas of being a faculty member were at odds with reality. His students were intransigent and incurious, the administrative part of his job was demanding and unreasonable productivity expectations kept him working all the time. Once he noticed how much he hated everything, he decided to leave. That was a hard decision for him, but he realized he was using himself to try to cover the gaps in the university, and it was wearing him out. Hitz also experienced alienation when she saw how empty university life was. She was upset by her participation in the performance and perpetuation of class. She had become materialistic, work-addicted, and egocentric. This wasn't what she had wanted at all—she had wanted a life of thinking.

Like both Malesic and Hitz, I had to remove myself from everything to find a way back to myself. Faced with writing my dissertation, I read books that comforted me. I wrote and wrote and wrote.

I struggled with working too much on the dissertation, of course, but in refusing to be with others, I still felt traces of guilt for focusing on my writing. I had always wanted to be a writer. Why had I given that up? While writing was stressful in many ways, after I left my social life behind, it became quieter. I discovered, in the quietness, a writing style that worked for me. I discussed this briefly in the last chapter as a response to misogyny. That voice didn't emerge until I spent more time alone, reading.

I had to learn to relate to myself differently. I focused on pleasure. I started listening to music. I hadn't listened to music for enjoyment (or at all, really) since I started my doctorate. I walked often. I tried to let go of striving. This was uncomfortable for me. It brought up an ugliness in myself. I berated myself for not working harder. I raged at my failures. Why couldn't I just tough it out like everyone else? Who was I to think I deserved time to myself to think? What was everyone thinking about me? These were all very self-centered thoughts! One of the violent parts of burnout is what Byung-Chul Han calls "auto-aggression." It refers to attacking yourself for not conforming to expectations about labor. And I did attack myself. I was my own worst critic. I complained about how the institution failed me and how it didn't value me as I was. But I didn't value myself either. I had no way to understand myself outside the work I did.

Another aspect of this is the profound isolation of burnout. It is different than solitude. Solitude is a chosen condition in which you gather yourself. Isolation is a forceful separation between you and others. Burnout undermines our ability to be present with others, imposing isolation through labor and competition. We fail, in the burnout condition, in friendship and political solidarity. Once I stepped back from everything, I started to connect with friends for quiet afternoons. My friendships blossomed during this time. I was more easily able to relate to people. I could pay attention to our conversations. I enjoyed hearing what others were doing. I no longer had to come up with a long critique or organizing campaign in response to someone's speech. When you are deep in the depths of struggling and laboring as an individual, you cannot connect with others. You can't throw your lot in with theirs. While I was doing activism, I had few meaningful relationships, and the work was soul-destroying.

Another way to combat burnout was connecting with myself through reading. Reading, especially novels, was the one time I could settle in to do this. Paradoxically, it allowed me to get out of myself. And that made it easier to see myself. If burnout is an excess of self, of activity and striving and laboring, reading cuts through that self-centeredness. For a little while, you can rest. You inhabit another person's mind. You see the world a little differently. You can also reflect on your own mind and world. The novels I read gave dignity and care to women harmed by the world. The novels showed misogyny and violence, but they also showed how women were more than their victimization. In *Milkman*, the narrator did her reading and walking. In *Girl, Woman, Other*, one character dances for no reason other than pleasure. In *Fleishman Is in Trouble*, the narrator steals time by running off alone. These pockets of solitude and pleasure carved out a space for a self not defined by others, just like reading did for me.

In this section, I've discussed healing from burnout through connecting to others and reading. Burnout is an isolating phenomenon, which makes struggling against it difficult. As a result, my suggestions here are less collective than in earlier chapters. This does not make it any less political. This individual work is just as important, especially if it prepares us for solidarity with ourselves and others. In the next section, I look at international conversations about burnout. This discourse has similar characteristics, focusing on the individual. The movement against overwork is implicitly collective, as individuals come to similar conclusions though they unfortunately seem to do so separately.

International conversations about burnout and conclusion

Burnout isn't just an American phenomenon. It is also not limited to universities. Unfortunately, though, most of the research on burnout comes from the US. It is also largely about the US and relatively privileged workers. This is a problem. Burnout can manifest differently for individuals based on context. That means strategies for fighting it also vary. Knowing about the struggles of others is a great way to fine-tune our understanding. In addition to the focus on the US, the research tends to skew middle class. Many commentators assume people can easily change jobs. They also suggest quitting for a while entirely. Not everyone can do that. We need to start collectively struggling around this issue. We cannot expect individuals to manage it on their own.

In this section, I want to consider other cultures, particularly those with vocal anti-work discourses. I look to China, South Korea, and Japan for that reason. South Korea and Japan have their own unique hierarchies that compound the problem of overwork and isolation. At the same time, they have similar capitalist economies to the US. In China, the pressure of conformity is an added stressor. Another unique feature is the Communist Party's censorship of dissent. This has been especially visible in their refutation of the lying flat movement, which I discuss below.

Students and workers in countries such as China, South Korea, and Japan (to name a few) experience burnout, too. In all of these cultures, there is intense pressure from one's parents to succeed. Young people also face a brutal job market. Competition within the university, as one workplace, is fierce. This gives rise to more and more work on the part of students. For example, in South Korea, they have cram schools. Students go to extra school to get ahead. They spend long hours at school under harsh supervision. Then they go to more school. In China, long work hours are a norm in the university. This has led to low satisfaction for faculty and staff, as well as burnout.

For Japanese students, similar demands for excellence and hard work are exhausting. Workdays are just as long in Japan as they are in Korea and China. Extended socializing with coworkers is expected after work. This means much of the time of young adults is captured in work time. This after work time is often based around drinking, meaning women often experience sexual harassment as part of these "social" outings. The intensity of social pressure in Japan has created a group of people named hikikomori. The English translation is roughly "those who are alone." Researchers argue hikikomori are everywhere, including in Italy, where social withdrawal has also risen. However, the phenomenon of young people withdrawing entirely is especially visible in Japan. They refuse to speak to their parents, to attend school, or to communicate with friends.

What young people learn in university in these cultures (and ours) is how to work at all costs. But the tides might be turning. Young workers all over the world have started saying no. They refuse to participate in a system that exhausts them. I'm particularly interested in the Chinese movement called tang ping (躺平) or "lying flat." The name comes from an essay by anonymous writer Luo Huazhong (the name translates to "Kind-Hearted Traveller"). The essay demonstrates that US academics aren't the only ones advocating for rest and retreat. The essay argues for a withdrawal from capitalist social life as a way to a better world. Lying flat means quitting work and lying around. Literally. It is a refusal of work, but also other forms of social life. It functions as a kind of performative protest. Huazhong argues that our consumptive lifestyle is related to the problem of overwork. So he avoids consuming at all costs. We can see an international connection in the phenomenon of "quiet quitting," too. A smaller refusal than lying flat, perhaps, but a refusal nonetheless.

All the discontent has provoked a backlash. The Chinese government has denounced younger workers as entitled and lazy. In America, we have a similar discourse. Pundits abuse millennials for protesting deteriorating working conditions and declining safety nets. Their rationale is that earlier generations suffered, so millennials should too. Denunciations of hikikomori are cruel, blaming them for their condition and attributing it to depression. Calling it depression depoliticizes the act of social withdrawal. It makes it medical rather than political. In general, blaming workers for their discontent is how the ruling class narrative works.

Another disheartening connection is the correlation between academic burnout and suicide, especially of young people. But this connection goes unmentioned in most books on burnout. It is a serious omission. There has been an increase or peak in suicides among students in all four countries (US, China, South Korea, and Japan). At my last university, we seemed to receive a suicide notice every other week. Now imagine that on a global scale. We need to better attend to the connections between mental health, class, and academic struggle. These connections show that burnout is not solely the domain of middle-class academics. It also shows us that this battle has high stakes. In their loneliness, those who are struggling make desperate decisions. We have lost people we will now never know as friends, lovers, and scholars. This is unacceptable.

Real, collective change seems to be out of reach. Contesting work and its conditions has historically been the province of unions. In the US, Petersen traces the evolution of burnout to the right-wing destruction of work protections. I would include here the Clinton administration's implementation of workfare. This undermined social safety nets for the unemployed by tying their eligibility to work or seeking it out. In any case, leisure time declined along with unions and labor power. Destroying unions replaces collective forms of bargaining with individual ones. Instead of a contract, you have to set boundaries with your abusive manager. (Ha!) The lack of union protections also characterizes China, South Korea, and Japan. Unions may be present, but they have, effectively, been defanged.

No one is alone in their burnout. This is an international phenomenon. Fighting burnout is, in part, a battle against ideas about work. We have internalized ideas harmful to us. This means our ways of working perpetuate the problem. Spending time connecting to ourselves is vital for healing from burnout. It is also vital for building connections with others. But we also need to recognize that the struggle is collective and about real working conditions. We may have individual things we need to do, but it is with others that we make true change. We have to collectively decide on a new definition of the good life. One that rejects work as a centerpiece. The costs are too high.

In this chapter, I have described burnout and different kinds of academic labor driving it. I have shown that significant changes need to be made. If we want to make the institution truly accessible to all, we have to do better. My discussion led to a consideration of contemplation as an antidote to burnout. In my final chapter, I turn to the thinking life promised by the university. I evaluate both its promises and its failures.

Discussion questions

1. What are your attitudes about work? Where did they come from?
2. Return to your answer about narrating your class background from the last chapter. How do you think it influences your approach to work?
3. Have you ever experienced burnout or tiredness in the work you have to do as a student or in any of your other roles in life? How do you feel about homework, essays, or exams? What is their cumulative effect on your college experience?
4. What kinds of self-care practices do you have? Why do you do those practices? What kinds of social care do you think they're replacing?

5.   Are you going to school for something you love? If so, what enables you to do this? If you're not, why not?

6.   If you're not a student, how do you feel about different aspects of work such as grading, spreadsheet-making, emailing, etc.? How do you feel about your work overall?

7.   Keep a journal of all the tasks you complete in a day. Try to keep it for a couple of days so you can get a good breadth of tasks. Which tasks do you feel are relevant to you? Which tasks do you enjoy? Do you have control over which tasks you complete and when? Why or why not? Is there anything you can do to get more autonomy? If you're a supervisor or a teacher, is there a way you can bestow more autonomy?

Recommended reading

Han, B.-C. (2015). *The Burnout Society*. Translated by Erik Butler. 2010. Stanford University Press.

Huazhong, L. "Tang Ping." Trans. Bugs (anonymous). Available at: https://chi.st/bugs/tang-ping [Accessed 11 March 2024].

Kim, R. C., Cahill, A. J. and Jacquart, M. (2020). Bearing the brunt of inequality: Ontological labor in the academy. *Feminist Philosophy Quarterly*, 6(1), pp. 1–27.

Malesic, J. (2022). *The End of Burnout: Why Work Drains Us and How to Build Better Lives*. University of California Press.

Petersen, A. H. (2020). *Can't Even: How Millenials Became the Burnout Generation*. Dey Street Books.

4
Finding my voice and thinking with others

The email from my adviser was brief:

This whole chapter needs to be rewritten.

After receiving my adviser's email, I despaired. Months of work had to be scrapped. I had to start the dissertation all over again. What if I couldn't do it? Even worse: I had been studying English for going on ten years! I had been reading my whole life. How did I make it this far without knowing how to write about literature?

My initial response was to blame myself. I didn't think about why I felt ill equipped to write a dissertation. I also didn't (consciously) realize that I needed to rescue my voice out from under the concerns of others. But when I went back and read the essay I had submitted, I didn't recognize the words at all. Who was speaking here? Why did I avoid naming my central concerns in favor of abstraction and historical analysis? Why didn't I just say **the character has an experience like mine?**

In the school of criticism I came from, the "I" was nowhere to be found. The historical context of a work was basically a god.

I could not, as far as I could tell, write literary criticism unless I used history to explain a book. Or I could use a book to illustrate a historical period (as I had done). It would have been the height of stupidity to say, "This book changed my outlook on life." That simply was not what books were for. I read novels to illustrate other people's ideas. I did not acknowledge any response the book caused in me, nor did I suggest that it affected me in any way. I wrote in the voice of others. I wrote in their style as well.

The process of writing that first chapter was worse than pulling teeth. I clawed each word out of a deep void. It took me several months to write the draft my mentor rejected. Three months of work down the drain. Weeks passed, and my despair deepened. I wrote nothing during that time. I was having a crisis of style—and of self.

In this chapter, I discuss classed and gendered expectations around research. Earlier, I described the effect of misogyny on knowledge production. I focused on the distress and the choice to write about misogyny itself. Now, I want to expand that discussion. In particular, I write about my struggle to find a voice. This struggle was related to the events I recounted in the earlier chapters. I also struggled against norms in scholarship that dictated what could be said—and by whom. In the final sections, I turn toward the pleasures of finding a voice and how we might transform writing within the university to be more democratic.

Searching for a voice: The dangers

After the blow of having my first chapter rejected, I had no idea how to move forward.

Finding my voice and thinking with others 75

How did this happen? To be honest, my voice had been missing for a long time. A teacher once commented on a paper that my "I" was vague and searching for something, but what I was looking for wasn't clear. I hadn't realized I was looking for something. I certainly acted as if I was. I constructed reading lists for exams based on a "canon" of women's literature. I read voraciously but was never full. I couldn't put what I read into any coherent form. Ultimately, I was looking for feminism and community. I needed a place to test my ideas and to be in conversation. I also needed more time to write. In between all my other obligations, I could only dedicate one hour a day to writing. That wasn't going to cut it. There was no way I could find more time in my day. Further, what was I going to say?

The university deprives us of our voices in many ways. In this section, I want to think about how hierarchy affects our thinking. It affects what we think about and whether we consider ourselves thinkers at all. This can be a problem of representation, where you don't see other thinkers like you. It can also be a problem of the dominant discourse, which erases many voices. Many practices limit what we can say and how. These same practices ensure a kind of homogeneity among thinkers in the academy.

Our voices in the university develop in the context of fear and domination. Grades are one form of threat, as is withholding an accreditation like a degree. As a teacher, I grew frustrated with students who refused to do creative work. Instead, they wanted to know what I wanted from them. In other words, they treated me as any other authority figure based on a mix of real and perceived harm. They were used to relating to teachers this way and probably had teachers who abused their authority. I also treated my teachers like this. I wanted my committee to tell me what they wanted. I wanted them to tell me what to do. I was worried I wouldn't get my degree otherwise. An equivalent feature of faculty life is peer review or tenure assessments. These kinds of evaluations, at all levels, stifle thought. They hamper individual and collective flourishing. The standards are punitive: do this or else. We can see here the implicit education that goes on in universities. We train people to be docile and fearful.

As an example, personal writing is often perceived as unprofessional. Teachers warned of this when I was a young writer. I learned to delete myself from papers. I contorted language to avoid the "I" rather than treating it as a hard-earned stylistic choice. I remember one comment saying no one would find me credible since I started a paper with an "I." That I was in my 20s and listened to this now irritates me. The professor meant well, but the comment stuck with me. To be clear, there are lazy ways of using an "I," typically from people who are not very self-reflective. But this laziness can also afflict so-called "impersonal" or academic writing. The judgments about "I" are often quick assumptions about a scholar's seriousness or their knowledge. But there are also preferences for subject matter. We know that hard sciences tend to command more respect than the so-called "soft" humanities. Oh, you wrote a book about your girlhood? Well, he just discovered a star. Even the distinctions we make are gendered.

Young women, especially working-class women who rely on different kinds of labor to get by are raised to have little confidence in their voices. Low expectations hamper your ability (and even your desire) to speak from yourself. Social context can teach you that your voice isn't as powerful. I learned this when confronted by male colleagues and more powerful professors. I learned this as a young girl when sons were preferred over daughters. We can even see this in citations in the university. Feminists have long documented the inequalities of citation, noting that women are likely to be less cited in general, though this varies based on race and class. Women are also less likely to cite themselves. I was also appalled, as a young writer, by the number of feminist thinkers whose entire framework relied on a male scholar. It seemed to go against feminist thinking and to avoid immersing oneself in that history. It also demonstrated that feminism itself was never sufficient. It was too shallow a pool to swim in. This is part of the gendering of academic thought.

Another obstacle is celebrity culture as it applies to the citation of scholars. I mentioned the culture of celebrity in Chapter One. This is a kind of devotion to relatively famous faculty. Such devotion immunizes them from accountability. It also treats them as a kind of idol, someone who deserves praise and recognition (at the cost of others). This isn't just something academics do with real people. It also shapes the culture of citation. Students' voices are often submerged under citations in a work. There is immense pressure to cite frequently and selectively. This is harmful because it outsources thinking to authority. This is helpful when learning to be in conversation with others.

But often such citation works to avoid conversation by reiterating who is important enough to cite or speak. Students are often required to attach every thought to a quote from someone else. These quotes are usually to provide evidence for an argument. Typically, this just means hiding behind the arguments of others. Think of all the academic work that claims to be a derivative of someone else. As an example, any scholar who describes themselves as "Foucauldian" does violence to their work. How? Because they try to use Foucault's name to garner authority and credibility instead of standing in their own voice. And it doesn't work. It just props up Foucault. You shouldn't be someone else's disciple. You should be your own thinker.

In any case, what this teaches a student is that they don't have any intuition or style of their own, at the level of prose or structure. We teach them not to believe in their voices. Instead, we hold up some scholars as eternal founts of wisdom rather than useful references that are more or less useful. But we don't do this. Instead, we prevent students from developing a unique style or voice. Rather than a malicious tendency, I think it's just easier than actually engaging with students' development. Further, what we call research is often limited to the idiom of the argument. We structure writing around a thesis and supportive points, engaging in conflict with other thinkers. As if the only way to account for the world were to argue about it. This discounts or erases other ways of writing about or engaging with oneself or the world.

When I was in school, I was often told, "You have to cite this thinker" or "Then you must talk about X topic." This got worse as I became a doctoral student. But because I was a student, I never questioned this. I just walked away feeling scolded. But then I would get confused. I would read the recommended thinker. I would research the recommended topic. And they had nothing to do with what I was interested in. I was paralyzed by this dilemma. By the time I got to my dissertation, I felt I had to please my committee, so I had to keep all this useless stuff in my chapters! It created a sense of inadequacy in my writing. I felt unable to write without recourse to other thinkers.

It's difficult to trace this insecurity back to one thing. It was gender but also class. The field of research I was interested in was full of thinkers considered minor. My ability to garner authority through citing feminists was fraught. It depended on the reader. Feminist thinkers earn a lot of ire and polarized reactions, so I felt I had to be careful (my conflict avoidance was still strong). I didn't command authority as a woman, either. I felt my intellectual ability was doubted or dismissed. My concerns were viewed as trivial. By working from my experience, I was trafficking in myself. This is the working-class girl's heritage, as Carolyn Kay Steedman has written. When that's all you have, you work with it. But the personal style was, as I said, risky.

To explain that better, I did not use the kind of reasoning that my faculty did. This was a matter of class mostly because I did not have the luxury to separate my life and my research. I also did not have the luxury to develop ideas over years and years. I had to write my dissertation quickly and with minimal support. No one in my family knew anything about academic research. I did not have the kind of community that provided rigorous feedback or helped me work through my ideas. Some fellowships provided this, but you had to compete to belong. Faculty also had these kinds of communities. They thanked them in their acknowledgments. I had friends I discussed my work with, but no one wrote about the same thing. I had the marginal comments on my chapters from committee members. One committee member even told me I wasn't demanding enough from my committee.

I didn't know how to ask for more. I just worked out my ideas alone. I didn't know what else to do.

Developing a voice, then, can be socially risky or outright dangerous. Class and gendered inequalities mean some people have less "access" to developing a voice. Middle-class and masculine strictures in writing include removing the "I", barring certain types of evidence, and employing methods of argumentation that obscure interests. These implicit rules, enforced by teachers or peer review, eradicate a variety of styles. These different styles could enrich and transform academic research. It would make research accessible to more people, both as writers and readers. It would also make research more relevant to the world. You can also imagine hiding your voice just to get through a program. After all, you're dependent on a more privileged faculty.

These are significant obstacles to navigate. Many people never overcome them. In this section, I have described features of academic life that can prevent finding a voice. We saw that hierarchies between teacher and student make style risky to develop. We also saw different practices in the university that police citation and style, like peer review. In the next section, I turn toward the pleasures and politics of finding one's voice. I use this section to inspire my concluding section. There, I think about how we might encourage more freedom of voice in the academy.

Finding my voice

I was at a breaking point. I realized the only way forward was to write what I knew and how I felt. I knew I had to write as I read, not as I had been taught to read. Further, I couldn't ignore the novels I was reading. They were helping me think about my daily life and my miserable university experience. It felt important to capture my thinking in light of those novels. I had to give up this image of my committee being forbidding. They hadn't told me I couldn't write as I was writing. If they didn't see the value of my work, that wasn't my fault. I also had to let go of searching for a topic that would somehow "land me a job" and write about what was in front of me. I had to use the voice I had. I couldn't keep wishing I had another. This decision coincided with my decision to step back from my social life.

In this section, I'm going to talk about finding my voice in my dissertation. I describe how that affected my personal life, too. I also want to note the relationships that supported me as I struggled through the (new) first chapter of my dissertation.

I knew rewriting the first chapter of my dissertation would be hard. I showed no one what I was writing. My voice is easily influenced by others. I didn't want to interact with someone only to be filled with doubt. I didn't want to be knocked off course. I had taken my advisor's advice and cleared my plate so I could focus on my writing. Even then, I dreaded trying to rewrite that chapter.

As I doubted my ability to go on, I found Cho Nam-Joo's *Kim Jiyoung, Born 1982*. The novel seemed to condense what I had been thinking about class and gender. The novel is masterful in its spare and page-turning representation of misogyny. It reveals how women's consciousness is deformed by patriarchy. The book also focuses on how personal relationships are a site of oppression for women. I abstractly knew this, but hadn't put it into words.

My first reading of that novel was fast. I was spellbound and read it in one sitting. I penciled a star next to every moment that was like my life. I wrote a couple of words to remind myself: "harasser," "bullies," "brothers preferred." There was also a unique feature of the novel that I couldn't stop thinking about. Kim Jiyoung speaks in the voices of dead women when she complains. It is a haunting ventriloquism, one that gets her sent to a psychiatrist. I recognized the metaphor but couldn't say why it was bothering me.

I felt I had been speaking in others' voices for so long. My partner and I got into an argument, one of our worst. As it dragged on, I realized with horror that *I sounded like someone else*. It wasn't my voice coming out of my body. And in my writing, I used other people's arguments to avoid describing my own. I reflected my professors' preferences back to them. Even with my friends, I stuck to subjects they cared about. Most of the time, I just swallowed my voice. Whose voice was this?

Reading *Kim Jiyoung, Born 1982* alarmed me. I was upset to see myself reflected in Kim Jiyoung's life. I was heartbroken that her husband ignored her wishes or pressured her into situations. I was devastated as she lost her sanity as a mother and as a worker. I didn't want my life to be like that. I would have to change, or my life would be lived on other people's terms. It, my life, seemed to be sliding out of my grasp. Along with my voice.

I didn't want to be like that. I was tired of being afraid to speak up for myself, whether at home or at school. Using my voice, in other words, would provoke others. But their reaction was not my responsibility. After that fight, I wrote what would become the first chapter of my dissertation in just a few weeks. It began with that argument as a sign that something was wrong. It was evidence of my struggles with my voice. But it cracked open all my other struggles, which you've been reading about in this whole book. I just kept writing and writing.

My essay moved between my experience and Kim Jiyoung's. I used her experience as evidence but also as a way to talk about my own life. Instances I never would have described as patriarchal suddenly became vivid to me. I connected my experiences at university with hers. I wrote that the book helped me see misogyny in the university and my personal life. It helped me see where I was refusing to stand up for myself. I wrote about how men were treated better than women everywhere in my life.

I described the bullying in the department. I described growing up in a culture where boys always had priority and freedom. I described a culture where women had to work so hard, whether in customer service or at home. The style was radically different from anything I had written. I couldn't deny my connection to the material. I was still speaking in another voice, that of the novel. But I had taken a step closer to my own perceptions and concerns. It would be good enough for now. I took a deep breath before I submitted it and then sent it in. The response from my dissertation adviser was yet again a single sentence: *I think you've found your voice!* I let out a huge exhale.

The pleasures and politics of finding a voice

Why does finding your voice matter? Most alienation in culture is the result of being ruled by others. While this subordination has material aspects that are well documented, I'm concerned with what it does to us in less material terms. After all, this domiantion deprives us of voice and autonomy. Finding and developing a voice is central to feminist politics. Feminists argue that women are not seen as individuals with unique capacities. They are treated as a mass population, exchangeable with one another. Finding a voice is one way to combat patriarchy. Further, the focus on the personal in feminist theory and writing is central to feminist critique. I had to speak up both in my personal life and at work to truly find a voice that wasn't hemmed in by fear. That's what I've been doing throughout this book. I start from personal experience to demonstrate the true stakes of my critique. Concepts are not just ideas. We also live them, even if we live beyond them.

In this section, I explain the pleasures and politics of finding a voice. I draw on the history of feminist consciousness-raising, arguing for an alternative understanding of education. Consciousness-raising refers to education that makes an individual aware of their oppression. Consciousness-raising also makes us aware of our agency. This feminist history helps me explain the stakes of my style of writing, which focuses on lived problems.

I mentioned earlier that the personal voice and tone in writing are often diminished. This is gendered and classed. Those who might speak in a personal tone are treated as less scholarly and intellectual. We also treat personal experiences as flat data in our culture. An experience serves as evidence that something happened. We act as if it's transparent what that something is. This diminishes the work of those who study experience. Experience is not self-evident. It requires study and is just as challenging in terms of style and composition as any other kind of subject. We have to explain an experience, what made it possible, and the vocabulary we use to talk about it is hard earned. It helps us see the social world much more clearly.

For feminist thinkers, the personal is a tool to investigate social and structural realities. You may have heard a slogan: "The personal is political." This phrase was coined by Kathie Sarachild. It appears in *The Feminist Revolution*, a collection of radical feminist writings from the 1970s. Around the same time, the Italian feminist group Milan Women's Bookstore Collective made similar arguments. They wrote that "what women suffer from, basically, is not speaking for themselves, not saying by themselves what they want, but saying it instead to themselves, with the words of others." You might remember Kim Jiyoung's ventriloquism here and my compulsive citation of others. Not speaking from yourself is a kind of social illness, according to the Milan Women. Women speak in the voices and concerns of others. They displace what they want because it makes them safer. This afflicts feminist politics as much as personal life. Indeed, the Milan Women noticed a fear of disagreement in feminist politics. There was a fear of being singular or unique. Women assumed that belonging to a collective guaranteed safety. The Milan Women realized collective politics had to enable women to speak from themselves, for themselves. It could not demand they speak in unison. It could not demand that they pay fealty to certain ideas. Instead, feminist politics would be better off helping women develop a voice.

There are feminists, however, such as Norma Alarcón, who disagree with the value of the subject of consciousness. Such a subject, in her view, is a white, Western construct that requires a lot of privilege. I partially agree. It does require privilege to inhabit or achieve consciousness. However, consciousness-raising has been used transgressively by subordinated groups all over the world. Even if it is a Western concept, it has been put to effective use by other cultures. Further, for Alarcón, the implied social reality of consciousness-raising is isolation and individualization. I think she's also right that individualism in US culture is tied to competition and a lack of care. But there is more than one way to be an individual. There is more than one way to be a self. The goal, for Alarcón, seems to be a vague collectivity that the Milan Women rejected long ago. No matter where they are, women are told they have to serve someone else's community. Patriarchy or feminism, it doesn't matter. In either case, a woman is not of value in herself. She is only what she can do for others. This is wrong. I think education can remedy the harm of this socialization. We can cultivate different kinds of subjectivities. We don't just have to continue with these subordinated ones.

I think that consciousness-raising gets us out of our isolation. It connects us to the world and others. It helps us become less self-centered. We realize we were never the origin of our suffering. When I was at my most isolated, I couldn't see beyond myself. I thought I had done something wrong. I thought that I had to work as hard as possible to get out of the hole. I didn't have the words "burnout", "labor", or "misogyny". As a result, the world had become impossible. What helped me was reading the novels for my dissertation. They were about the diminishment of women in capitalist, patriarchal, conservative, and violent contexts. These were contexts, in other words, where speaking from oneself was dangerous. Equally, for these characters, not speaking from themselves also caused considerable pain. These fictional characters couldn't change anything, but I could.

I didn't disappear into myself as I stepped back to write my dissertation. Instead, I reached outwards. I explored the meaning of feminism to me. I blossomed into new relationships. Every week, my friend R and I met to write together for a few hours. We refused any other demands on our time. With my friend K, I took walks and discussed new books. We brought up feminist ideas we were interested in. With my friend C, I wrote articles about university education and politics. My friend R and I debated literary theory until we couldn't stop laughing. These relationships made me feel real. It wasn't a world bound by family or waged work, two energy-sapping traps. I started to divest from subjectivities that did not help me.

My mentor also provided key support as I wrote. She modeled the kind of writing and intellectual life I wanted. She also held space for me to mess up, clarify what I thought, and figure out how to overcome obstacles. I chose her as my mentor because I admired her style. She wrote in the first person! And she taught feminist theory. She was the first teacher I had who evaluated my style of writing. She drew attention to my (unconscious) writing choices as indicative of my political concerns. Such an evaluation gave me back some agency over my writing in an important way. She was also very skilled at keeping negative space where I could learn and grow on my own. While sometimes I hoped for more connection with her, I am a people pleaser. I need time on my own to develop ideas; otherwise, I will be monitoring others for how they feel. This can influence what I'm arguing. By holding space where I had to figure things out by myself, she made me responsible for my education. She was able to give me what I needed, not necessarily what I wanted. That is, in itself, a gift.

My experience revealed just how vital other women were to finding my voice. Teachers, friends, authors, and literary characters all helped me. A community doesn't just have to be physical people. I was immersed in a feminist community older and more stable than I had previously thought. It was people but also an intellectual tradition. Education is a collective endeavor that the individual takes part in and furthers. It builds on the past. Seeking your voice, ideally, helps others find theirs. I was lucky to have teachers and friends guiding me and rooting me on. My journey required care and attention. I was given both with no real ability to repay that gift. These women took my work and my value for granted. I no longer had to struggle to justify my work or my existence. I was valued simply as I was; and this is a gift that can never be repaid. Through these relationships, I became myself. I did not do so in isolation.

In this section, I have detailed the pleasures of my relationships in developing my voice. I also documented feminist arguments over consciousness-raising. I did so to illustrate the stakes of taking consciousness-raising as our model for education. This model of education turns us away from the university's typical modes of operation. It is a more grassroots, people-centered model that, I think, everyone could benefit from.

International and historical alternatives

But who has time (or money) for the experience I'm describing here? I spent ten years in school between all my degrees.

I accumulated debt. I worked other jobs and saved to support myself when I didn't have work in the summer. So much of our lives militates against time for contemplation. An obligation-filled life makes the fruits of thinking difficult to benefit from. Thinking also takes a long time. I started writing about feminist concerns in 2013. My voice and thinking didn't come to fruition until seven years later. This is not accessible to everyone. We're better off looking toward how to support thinking communities beyond the university. Education cannot and should not solely happen in institutions. Thankfully, it doesn't.

There are many traditional worker schools and many part-time institutions for the working class to attend higher education courses. These schools can serve as historical inspiration here. England, for example, has a rich worker education tradition. Marxist thinkers like Raymond Williams taught for Oxford's adult education program and the Workers' Educational Association. Both programs provided education for what we would now call non-traditional students. Virginia Woolf was involved in women's groups in the countryside of England. These groups provided education and community for women who were, at that time, excluded from university.

Consciousness-raising actions or groups are a worldwide feminist tradition. See, again, Hawon Jung's work and Leta Hong Fincher's work for examples from South Korea and China. The Milan Women's Bookstore Collective's book *Sexual Difference* recounts the experience of these groups of women in Italy. But they also write about what were called 100-hour schools for those seeking part-time, affordable education. Both provided an intellectual community.

In Chile, a group called LasTesis does feminist consciousness-raising through performance art. This art engages the community. The crowd participates, learning about feminist issues while developing their agency. While the group themselves are college-educated, their events and protests are for everyone. They stage performances that communicate feminist ideas in a format that empowers the community. In Brazil, we can point to the history of Paulo Freire's experimental critical pedagogy, which brought literacy to workers in both large- and small-scale formats outside of the university, even if Freire's position was within the Brazilian government.

In a US context, I teach writing classes outside the university. I work with a writing center that offers skill-building classes for writers of all backgrounds focused on many different topics. My courses focus on reading feminist works as a way back to the self and a way into writing. I focus on women writers who illuminate women's experiences, of oppression and otherwise. These classes are taken by women trying to find their writing voices. They are often trying to get back to themselves. The class offers a space for them to simply dwell on their words without any demands, hierarchy, or fear. I use women's writing as a way to raise consciousness in these classes and my sexual harassment prevention work. I hope to help students embody their voices, providing guidance and a safe space to do so. Class time allows them to step back from the demands and realities of life. It takes time and courage to rediscover who you are. I feel my work is to bring the feminist education I received to others. This kind of education should not be restricted to the university.

The kinds of contexts I'm noting here eradicate some of the hierarchical aspects of education. There are no grades, no outcomes, and no punitive forces. Even the small group is an improvement from the classes that usually have thirty or more students. While at the writing center students still have to pay for courses, they are much more affordable compared to a university degree. In performance art, like that done by LasTesis, you don't pay anything and are in relation with your community. You are also contesting hierarchy beyond and within the community. These examples show the global search for meaningful and democratic education. It gives us examples to draw on as we reimagine what education and thinking in a community can look like. No longer is the isolated scholar our only model—nor should she be.

I agree with scholar Zena Hitz that contemplation is as important as cooking, cleaning, or garbage collecting. But we don't act like it. Our culture starves those parts of us that are not immediately available for work or use. We are blindly materialist in our assessments of what makes a good life. We need to create spaces to feed those hungry parts of us, the parts that cannot be satisfied by commodities. We crave community *and* autonomy. We want the chance to think about questions that matter to us and our loved ones. Ultimately, finding a voice, or wielding an "I," is about staking a claim on the world-making aspect of politics. Politics isn't simply legislative or institutional. It's also how we organize our lives and time. It's how we value people and their work. A fully democratic and free culture can be achieved if everyone can use their favored capacities. This would mean recognizing each person as unique with varied interests. You couldn't just slot them into types to fulfill labor market demands.

This chapter is about my search for a voice and a community. It is also about the friends and mentors who helped me with that process. Countertraditions within the university, such as feminism, can be used to transform education. We need more humane, individual-centered models of learning if we want to create a truly free and democratic world. In this way, my story isn't just about a single, struggling learner. It's about what is at stake when the university fails us all.

Discussion questions

1.   Which parts of the university feel most empowering and generative to you? Describe them as best you can through personal experience. How can you make more of your university experience revolve around those parts? How can you include others in those empowering and generative aspects?

2.   Why does it matter to have a community to think with? Who in your life provides a safe space for you to think out loud and work out your ideas?

3.   What books or ideas have you encountered in the university that you think are important? How are you going to communicate those ideas beyond the university?

4.   Do you know what matters most to you as a skill or sense of purpose? Are you currently pursuing it? Why or why not? If you are pursuing it, what has enabled you to do so? If you're not, what has prevented you?

5.   If you ran an education program or developed an intellectual community, what would it be about? What do you think would foster the growth of those in the program or who are thinking with you?

Recommended reading

Grande, S. (2018). Refusing the University. In: E. Tuck and K. Wayne Yang, eds., *Toward What Justice?: Describing Diverse Dreams of Justice in Education*. Routledge, pp. 47–65.

Hitz, Z. (2020). *Lost in Thought: The Hidden Pleasures of the Intellectual Life*. Princeton University Press.

Harney, S. and Moten, F. (2013). *The Undercommons: Fugitive Planning and Black Study*. Autonomedia.

Rancière, J. (1991) *The Ignorant Schoolmaster: Five Lessons in Intellectual Emancipation*. Translated by Kristin Ross. Stanford University Press.

Woolf, V. (1957). *A Room of One's Own*. 1929. Harcourt Brace.

Conclusion

Transforming the university and education

Throughout this book, I have written about different forms of inequality within the university. I have also documented efforts to change it. My examples are from a particular place and time. These are only a few examples of political change and of the particular problems we face within universities. I emphasized creative thinking that confronts injustice in our daily lives. I illustrated connections between struggles against misogyny, racism, and workplace domination. In doing so, I'm not telling you what you should do; I am just showing different avenues you might take. If a particular struggle or discrimination does not appear here, do not take it as indifference but as the necessary limitation of one person in a particular place and time. I hope that you find, in the gaps, the story that only you can tell.

All universities are different, so it's tough to list exhaustive changes. Even within a university, different groups have different interests. Graduate students going on strike means undergraduates don't get grades on time. Faculty in one department may use their privilege to prevent a union for other university faculty. Janitorial staff need a raise, but management says there's no money. Management, instead, blames it on graduate students negotiating their contracts. Complaints of racism may proliferate in one department, but in another, there are numerous complaints of sexual harassment. This means there are different priorities and different organizing tactics in those departments.

Our current political moment has chilled political consciousness. It's easier to keep your head down and do your work without concern for others. It's less risky to talk about trending news items than to fight alienation where we are. In the last chapter, I argued that everyone needs time to think. I also think that everyone needs autonomy to make decisions for themselves. I admitted to turning away from political involvement to write my dissertation. But we do have a basic responsibility to others.

However, this responsibility is difficult to act on in the university. I want to acknowledge that political activity within universities is hard. Even beyond my examples, there are many obstacles. Awards, fellowships, and tenure incentivize individualism. There are examples of scholars and staff fired for their political speech. This creates a context of self-preservation. For example, I recently worked at a women's center. I advocated for a solidarity statement in light of the Supreme Court overturning **Roe v. Wade**. I argued that we needed to acknowledge this political reality, as a women's center. This turned out to be difficult. The fear was that we would all be fired, and our center defunded. So after much vetting, we released a vague statement I did not care for. When I was in a union, such a statement would have been easy. In a university with no unions and in a right-to-work state, I had few, if any, protections.

More broadly, we should organize education outside the university. This is not to say that education outside the university will be perfect. But what happens if we start from the belief that education belongs to all of us? What happens if we think of education as an end in itself? Competitive behaviors could vanish. We could take more pleasure in each other's company. We could think without fear. What would education look like if every individual mattered?

Below are some recommendations based on my thinking throughout this book. The first part of the list addresses the university. The last few suggestions address the position of education within the US as a whole. Those recommendations are much broader in scope. I feel they are appropriate. Most of the problems I discuss do not originate in the university. Thus, we have to look beyond it for changes. There are other ways to improve education besides these suggestions if we think creatively enough. What changes would transform your college experience?

1. Unionizing is a significant step forward. Unions can make changes within and beyond a university. Union drives can take years. Those years are important. They involve building community and honing political skills. Recent conservative attacks on universities suggest the value of unions. In Texas, the legislature banned diversity initiatives and education. Many lost their jobs as a result. Controlling the curriculum means controlling the narrative. It sends a clear message that college education belongs to the privileged, not to the masses. Unions provide a basis for contesting this message. They can also foster grassroots movements to prevent these power grabs. They can raise wages (crucial), ensure

retaliation protections, and protect workers' leisure time. These are just a few examples of things we need more of!

2.   Departments should introduce standards of conduct. While the university has standards of conduct, department-level work can be informal. This could be accomplished with regular meetings to increase connection. Meetings with all levels (faculty, staff, students) could build solidarity. The focus here is not punishment. Instead, the whole department would work toward creating a better environment. What if a department were a place to connect with fellow workers? What if we could decrease isolation? How do we foster comfort so individuals can disclose ongoing harm?

3.   There need to be consequences for misogynistic, racist, and homophobic behavior. Departments can present themselves as clear moral authorities on these issues, especially when it comes to abusive faculty. I have seen too many faculty members protected after disclosures of racism or sexual assault. Even among graduate students, these behaviors go unremarked. While I am not necessarily interested in punishing everyone, I would like consequences to be shifted from survivors to perpetrators. Those who experience racism and misogyny should be able to approach a department or reporting resource without fear of reprisal. It is reasonable to expect a remedy from a department on this issue, especially as it created an environment that allowed this behavior in the first place.

4.   Creating clearer standards of justice within the university, including recourse to a third party. Universities, for the most part, adjudicate their cases internally. This is true for Title IX cases. Title IX was initially a tool to challenge sexist

discrimination. In practice, many Title IX decisions are made to protect the university. There are few fair outcomes for those who seek its help. There is no other authority to appeal to. Working with my union, we could seek outside opinions. If we had an unfair grievance outcome, we could challenge that decision. The arbitration involved a truly neutral third-party investigator. The investigator could issue an independent decision. This usually turned the decision in our favor. A neutral arbiter of justice could level the playing field.

5.   Democratic control over university decisions. This should include the budget. Spending and curriculum changes should involve multiple groups. It shouldn't be up to boards of governors or legislators. It is unacceptable that decisions about university life are made by those who do not live it. Further, a poor understanding of university budgets causes confusion. For example, they can raise tuition with no tangible evidence of financial health. Universities claim they have no money when it comes time to give raises. They make similar claims when they decide to raise tuition. This basic lack of financial accountability is a stumbling block.

6.   Transforming funding for research and graduate education. Sandy Grande has argued for refusing awards and fellowships. This refusal means involving ourselves in collective politics. Funding through fellowships and grants exacerbates so many problems. It encourages competition and a self-centered approach to research. This also creates the problem of "institutional housework." Some scholars, in other words, don't receive grants. They ensure a department continues to run. They support students through grievances. We need to come up with better ways

to recognize good scholarly work beyond writing books and articles, including work that has nothing to do with publishing a book. The focus on accolades can be harmful in other ways. For instance, I know many women who watched their perpetrator receive grants for their work. At the same time, these women were leaving or downshifting to survive. Finally, awards contribute to celebrity culture. Harassment goes hand in hand with celebrity culture. Some are empowered to inflict power on others.

7. Better advising for students, at every level of education. This should include mentorship for faculty and staff to become good advisors. This has several effects. First, it creates good jobs. These jobs directly support the educational mission of the university. If we have to redirect funding from elsewhere, so be it. Second, it eases workloads. Faculty members would not have to support multiple students in addition to their other work (as is now the case). Third, it can help level the playing field. Inequality often reproduces because no one is paying attention. So many students fall through the cracks because of inadequate advising. This includes both advising on courses and advising on dissertations. My suggestion works against advising consolidation. This has happened at many universities. Three advisers are chosen for a college of thousands—a cost-saving measure. The university is choosing to fail students. First-generation students and those who transfer from community colleges are uniquely hurt by this.

8. Free college education and debt forgiveness. This is one example of looking beyond the university for changes that would improve university life. It would ease the struggles of many students across all different identities. Free education

would make college more accessible to folks who could not afford it before. So many would benefit: those working multiple jobs to get by, first-generation students, and poor folks. It would ease debt burdens and financial anxiety. Such a measure requires a national, grassroots effort. It could be easier to win tuition-free college at a state or local level first. and then use that momentum to transform the country. Debt forgiveness should be a part of this strategy. This measure, like free education, incurs conservative ire. It can also create resentment. Folks in my life complained about debt forgiveness. They had to pay their debt. So, they reasoned, why should someone else get relief? This is a good example of negative solidarity. We need real solidarity to change things. I paid student loans for a long time. I don't want anyone to have to do that. See how easy that was?

9. Autonomous public education. Some nonprofits already do this. The examples that come to mind focus on bringing skills to the public. Writing centers like Hugo House Center for Writers or Redbud Writing Initiative are good examples. They offer writing classes for a fraction of the cost of a college education. Local organizations like Merlin (in Helena, MT) and Durham Night School (in Durham, NC) offer affordable courses in philosophy. More creativity could lead to other, similar organizations for various fields.

10. Universal basic income. This measure would support all others. Universal basic income would provide a monthly stipend to everyone living in the United States. By providing for basic needs, it increases freedom and autonomy. Having a universal basic income means less fear and domination at work. It also means more freedom in choosing work

or going back to school. This, like free college education, requires grassroots work beyond the university.

I haven't even begun to scratch the surface. There are issues my list does not address partially because I'm not sure how to tackle them and partially because I'm not necessarily the person to write about them. The point is to dream big. From there, we can organize with one another.

These changes will not be easy. Those of us who want these things have to get organized. The wealthy, after all, benefit from our indebtedness and our work ethic. How else would they have an obedient workforce? Our competition with each other also benefits them. Transforming the university means undermining privilege that rests on the suffering of others. Even within the university, we will meet resistance. Male faculty typically contest diversity education, and they are successful in dislodging it. Wage hikes for the majority of workers mean less money for those at the top. This is just as true in a university. They want to pay us as little as possible. It increases their power and allows them to funnel money into military research, president salaries, and football stadiums. None of these things are necessary for human happiness or education.

What are the next steps? To conclude the book, I'm going to teach a critical thinking exercise I used to teach organizers (and that my union mentor taught me). To imagine change, you have to learn how to flip a problem. The flipping exercise is a method of power analysis. Overwhelmed by the change needed, people give up. How do we break it into bite-sized pieces? How do we turn our big dreams into different steps? We have to find concrete steps from the big dreams. These smaller goals sustain organizing work in the long run. We can rack up wins and avoid burnout using these small goals. I'm going to walk you through a power analysis "flip" exercise below. This exercise turns complaints into problems we can solve. We need more thinking like this. Together, we really can change things.

Power analysis exercise

1. Make a list like mine above: What things would you want to change about the university and why? Think back to the discussion questions in earlier chapters. Your answers probably gave you a list of problems you could analyze.

2. Take something you want to change about the university and flip it: What would it look like if your problem were "solved"? This is a tough exercise because you need to flip it exactly or the exercise won't work. See my example below for a template.

3. What would change about day-to-day life if you made your change? What positive or negative things would happen?

4. How would you go about making the change you have identified above? Who else would want to work on this problem with you? What power do you have to make the changes real? Power isn't just numbers or a bullhorn; it can also be skills that you have that could convince others to make the change or to become involved.

5. Who has a vested interest in preventing your goal from becoming real? Why do they hold that interest? What power do they hold to prevent you?

6. What strategy would you use to go about your change?

7. What would success look like?

Example power analysis

1. Sexual harassment causes women to drop out of college.

2. Sexual harassment does not cause women to drop out of college.

3. Women would have a supportive environment where perpetrators are easily reported, their harmful behavior is stopped, and no retaliation occurs. Women would finish school and enjoy their education.

4. I would begin with my department, where I know harassment is happening. I would talk to other women in the department, including key faculty, to ensure I have support. We have the power of numbers to make a change. We also have skills such as writing, presenting, teaching, and designing flyers. We can use all of these to our advantage.

5. Department leadership might not want to hold sexual harassers accountable due to fear of retaliation and Title IX restrictions. This means the Title IX office would also hold power. They ensure the university and department operations are not interrupted. They are bound to the institution's interest, not the interest of the faculty, staff, or students. These two groups will sometimes act to preserve power, but sometimes they can be allies. It depends on the relationships.

6. Our group could design zines to get the word out about our experiences of harassment to others around campus who might support us. (This grassroots work is key!) In addition, we can write a letter detailing our experiences, make a list of needed changes, and finish it with signatures from those in support and those affected by the issue. We can deliver the letter to the chair of our department. This part is

tricky as the chair may not have power, so we may have to go to the dean. Another way to build pressure is to publish an op-ed. The student paper is a good place to let the campus know this is unfolding. Sometimes, you could even try a bigger newspaper (if you have a good story). Even if we do not win, it will be known around campus that we were actively thwarted by our department/college.

7.   At the beginning stage, success would mean a concrete commitment from the department (and university) to hold perpetrators accountable. They would also need to demonstrate how they will create an environment safe for women. An appointed person would talk with those accused of harassment to communicate the discomfort they are causing and get them resources for better social skills. Further, creating spaces for women-only gatherings could be helpful. You might have other examples of what could make a harassment-free environment!

You can use this exercise many times over. Think about problems you face as solvable conundrums rather than fixed truths. Talk to those around you. Find a way forward together.

References

Ahmed, S. (2021). *Complaint!* Duke University Press.

Ahmed, S. (2019). On Complaint. YouTube. https://www.youtube.com/watch?v=4j_BwPJoPTE [Accessed 9 July 2024].

Alarcón, N. (1991). The theoretical subject(s) of this bridge called my back and Anglo-American Feminism. In H. Calderón and J. D. Saldivar, eds., *Criticism in the Borderlands: Studies in Chicano Literature, Culture, and Ideology*. Duke University Press, pp. 28–39.

Ali, T. (2023). University Staff in the UK are Refusing to Grade Students Work. *Jacobin*, 3 July 2023, https://jacobin.com/2023/07/higher-education-marking-assessment-boycott-neoliberalism-students-degree [Accessed 9 July 2024].

American Association of University Women. (n.d.). Fast Facts: Women Working in Academia. https://www.aauw.org/resources/article/fast-facts-academia/ [Accessed 14 April 2024].

Barnes, J. (2023). Melbourne University Workers are Getting Ready for a Second Week Strike. *Jacobin*, 29 September 2023, https://jacobin.com/2023/09/university-of-melbourne-nteu-casual-workers-strike [Accessed 9 July 2024].

Battistoni, A. (2019). Spade Work. N+1, Iss. 34, Spring, https://www.nplusonemag.com/issue-34/politics/spadework/[Accessed 12 Mar 2024].

Becker, K. D. (2019). Graduate students' experience of plagiarism by their professors. *Higher Education Quarterly*, 73, pp. 251–265.

Cech, E. A. (2021). *The Trouble with Passion: How Searching for Fulfillment at Work Fosters Inequality*. University of California Press.

Cho, N.-J. (2020). *Kim Jiyoung, Born 1982*. 2017. Trans. Jamie Chang. Liveright.

Chu, A. L. (2018). I Worked with Avital Ronnell. I Believe Her Accuser. Chronicle of Higher Education, August 30, 2018, https://www.chronicle.com/article/i-worked-with-avital-ronell-i-believe-her-accuser/ [Accessed 7 June 2021].

Conover, A. C. and Wallet P. (2022). We must pay attention to the West Africa's teacher strikes. *Teacher Task Force*, https://teacherta skforce.org/blog/we-must-pay-attention-west-africas-teacher-strikes [Accessed 9 July 2024].

Cruz, C. (2021). *The Melancholia of Class: A Manifesto for the Working Class*. Repeater Books.

Ernaux, A. (2016). *A Girl's Story*. Seven Stories Press.

Empowering Prevention and Inclusive Community. (2021). Equity Survey. https://www.washington.edu/safecampus/epic-program/

Empowering Prevention and Inclusive Community. (2019). EPIC 1.0 Curriculum. Original version created and edited by Paige Sechrest, Sam Sumpter, Kiana Swearingen with input from UAW 4121 members.

Empowering Prevention and Inclusive Community. (2020). EPIC 2.0 Curriculum. Original version created by Sam Sumpter and revised by Kaelie Giffel.

Evaristo, B. (2019). *Girl, Woman, Other*. Black Cat Press.

Freire, P. (2018). *Pedagogy of the Oppressed*. 1968. Trans. Myra Bergman Ramos. Bloomsbury.

Giffel, K. and Thorp, L., presiders. (2021). First-Generation Ph.D.s in the Academy. Modern Language Association Roundtable. Lindsey N. Chappell, Douglas Dowland, Brittney Michelle Edwards, Amber P. Hodge, Ana Maria Jimenez-Moreno, and Almas Khan, participants. 10 January 2021. Zoom session.

Grande, S. (2018). Refusing the University. In: E. Tuck and K. W. Yang, eds., *Toward What Justice?: Describing Diverse Dreams of Justice in Education*. Routledge, pp. 47–65.

Han, B.-C. (2015). *The Burnout Society*. Translated by Erik Butler. 2010. Stanford University Press.

Harney, S. and Moten, F. (2013). *The Undercommons: Fugitive Planning and Black Study*. Autonomedia.

Hollis, L. P. (2015). Bully University: The Cost of Workplace Bullying and Employee Disengagement in American Higher Education. *Sage Open*, pp. 1–11.

Hitz, Z. (2020). *Lost in Thought: The Hidden Pleasures of the Intellectual Life*. Princeton University Press.

Kandasamy, M. (2020). *When I Hit You: Portrait of the Writer as a Young Wife*. Europa Editions.

Kang, H. (2023). *Another Person*. Pushkin Press.

Kelly, B. T. (2019). Though More Women are on College Campuses, Climbing the Professor Ladder Remains a Challenge. *Brookings Institute*, 29 March 2019, https://www.brookings.edu/blog/brown-center-chalkboard/2019/03/29/though-more-women-are-on-college-campuses-climbing-the-professor-ladder-remains-a-challenge/ [Accessed 29 April 2022].

Kim, Ruthanne Crapo, Ann J. Cahill, Melissa Jacquart. (2020). Bearing the Brunt of Inequality: Ontological Labor in the Academy. *Feminist Philosophy Quarterly,* 6(1), pp. 1–27.

LasTesis. (2023). *Set Fear on Fire: the Feminist Call that Set the Americas Ablaze*. Verso Books.

Lau, Y.-W. (2024). *Tongueless*. Trans. J. Feeley. Feminist Press.

Malesic, J. (2022). *The End of Burnout: Why Work Drains Us and How to Build Better Lives.* University of California Press.

Manne, K. (2017). *Down Girl: The Logic of Misogyny*. Oxford University Press.

Milan Women's Bookstore Collective. (1997). *Sexual Difference: A Theory of Social Symbolic Practice*. Trans. Teresa de Lauretis. Routledge.

Mitchell, N. (2019). Summertime Selves (On Professionalization). *New Inquiry*, October 4, 2019, https://thenewinquiry.com/sum mertime-selves-on-professionalization/ [Accessed 7 June 2021].

Mitchell, N. (2020). The View from Nowhere: On Frank Wilderson's Afropressism. *Spectre*. Fall, pp. 110–122.

Nash, J. C. (2019). *Black Feminism Reimagined: After Intersectionality*. Duke University Press.

Petersen, A. H. (2020). *Can't Even: How Millennials Became the Burnout Generation*. Dey Street Books.

Prescod-Weinstein, C. (2021). *The Disordered Cosmos: A Journey into Dark Matter, Spacetime, and Dreams Deferred*. Bold Type Books.

Rancière, J. (1991). *The Ignorant Schoolmaster: Five Lessons in Intellectual Emancipation*. Trans. Kristin Ross. Stanford University Press.

Sarachild, K. The Personal is Political. In *Feminist Revolution*, Redstockings of the Women's Liberation Movement, ed. 1975. Random House.

Sparrow, J. (2022). In Australia, Precarious University Workers are Stepping Up the Fight. *Jacobin*, April 2022, https://jacobin.com/2022/04/academia-precarious-university-workers-australia-union-organizing-casuals-nteu [Accessed 9 July 2024].

Spoon, K., LaBerge, N., Wapman, K. H., Zhang, S., Morgan, A. C., Galesic, M. Fosdick, B. K., Larremore, D. B. and Clauset, A. (2023). Gender and Retention Patterns Among U.S. Faculty. *Science Advances*, 9, pp. 1–12.

Steedman, C. K. (1987) *Landscape for a Good Woman: A Story of Two Lives*. Routledge.

Tagba, K. (2022). Togo Dismisses More Teachers in Dispute with Teacher's Union. *Aljazeera*, https://www.aljazeera.com/news/2022/4/7/togo-dismisses-more-teachers-in-fresh-row-with-teachers-union [Accessed 9 July 2024].

Vattese, T. (2019). Sexism in the Academy: Women's Narrowing Path to Tenure. N+1(34) https://www.nplusonemag.com/issue-34/essays/sexism-in-the-academy/ [Accessed 13 Mar 2024].

Williams, R. (1981). *Politics and Letters: Interviews with New Left Review*. Verso Books.

Woolf, V. (1957). *A Room of One's Own*. 1929. Harcourt Brace.

Woolf, V. (1963). *Three Guineas*. 1938. Mariner Books.

Index

www.ingramcontent.com/pod-product-compliance
Lightning Source LLC
Chambersburg PA
CBHW071748270326
41928CB00013B/2843